THE
AMERICANIST

THE

AMERICANIST

DANIEL AARON

THE UNIVERSITY OF MICHIGAN PRESS

ANN ARBOR

Copyright © by Daniel Aaron 2007
All rights reserved
Published in the United States of America by
The University of Michigan Press
Manufactured in the United States of America
⊚ Printed on acid-free paper

2010   2009   2008   2007   4   3   2   1

A CIP catalog record for this book is available from the British Library.

Library of Congress Cataloging-in-Publication Data

Aaron, Daniel, 1912–
    The Americanist / Daniel Aaron.
        p.   cm.
    Includes index.
    ISBN-13: 978-0-472-11577-8 (cloth : alk. paper)
    ISBN-10: 0-472-11577-4 (cloth : alk. paper)
    1. Aaron, Daniel, 1912–   2. Historians—United States—Biography
3. Historiography—United States.   4. United States—Study and
teaching.   5. United States—Politics and government—20th century—
Miscellanea.   6. Presidents—United States—History—20th century—
Miscellanea.   7. Critics—United States—Biography.   8. American
literature—History and criticism.   I. Title.

E175.5.A15A3   2007
973.072'02—dc22   2006025450

for Benjamin Aaron

Among the many to whom I'm indebted for information and counsel, I thank my editor and longtime friend, Jeannette Hopkins, who gave *The Americanist* its most rigorous going over.

I also thank especially Norman Mackenzie, Christoph Irmscher, Lewis M. Dabney, David H. Donald, Arthur M. Schlesinger Jr., Justin Kaplan, Eugene Goodheart, Werner Sollors, Joel Porte, and Helen Vendler, who read all or parts of the manuscript and offered useful suggestions. I owe much to other friends and colleagues (among them William Doering, Sacvan Bercovitch, Warner Berthoff, Philip Fisher, Jim Sleeper, and Donald Fanger) who served as sounding boards for this reminiscence.

Susannah Tobin, unfailingly attentive, expertly computerized the manuscript.

. . . a Book wherein I write everything, as I see it
or as my thoughts suggest it to me.
—G. C. LICHTENBERG

WRITER TO READER

On February 16, 1896, Samuel Butler wrote to his father, "If I had a friend to advise in early life, I should say, 'change your name to Aaron,' and you will be pretty safe to head all alphabetical lists.'" That happened to be mostly true in my case, save on the rare occasions when I was bumped out of alphabetical ascendancy by a stray Swede or Korean. I gained no advantage from my surname, God knows, and quickly learned to distinguish the alphabetical "Daniel Aaron," usually assigned the first seat in the first row of the schoolroom, from his erratic and subterranean double.

In this narrative, I am the Americanist, who gradually evolves into a practitioner of things American. I liken him to a Christian child planted by his Turkish captors into an elite corps of Janissaries; or to an animal who has survived by protective mimicry; or to an anonymous character who has seeped into the minds of his friends, associates, and enemies. Perhaps traces of him can still be found where he once lived or spoke or visited—places as diverse and far apart as Tulsa and Beijing, South Bend and Helsinki, Carbondale and Sao Paulo; as Hokaido, Montevideo, Warsaw, Sydney, Delhi, and Belfast. He is snagged in a thousand snapshots and, like Whitman, feels himself to be a part of the unconscious scenery of a thousand more. Although he can't, as Whitman could, project himself back to the time when he was an egg carried in the mouth of a dinosaur, he does insinuate himself into a web of history that extends from Greece and Rome to George

W. Bush. He is the familiar "I" and the voices of the following other selves:

The naïf—pockmarked by the events he has lived through in the last century but with only a limited comprehension of the economic and scientific machinery that has transformed the world since his birth. In this respect he is like most of his countrymen. Unlike many of them, however, he hasn't outgrown an adolescent simplicity and is easily bamboozled.

The young man—on occasion solipsistic, sentimental, ironical, scornful, arrogant, rebellious, and operatic, though seldom so in public. Orphaned at an early age, he is a father seeker, hungry for acceptance, eager to slough off his Jewish identity and to melt into the larger America. The worldliness and sophistication he affects (Leopardi's pessimism, Anatole France's ironies, Huysmans's decadence, Nietzsche's paganism) are at odds with an abiding social timidity. His pretensions are cosmic/comic.

The national representative—designated mouthpiece for his country in foreign parts, expounder of its history and literature, and (in the nomenclature of the Soviet Union) a "cultural imperialist." He pays short and lengthy visits to Western and Eastern Europe and to Japan and China, the Middle East, Latin America, Australia, India—his subject being American literature and society. Far from concealing the blemishes of the United States on these tours, he feels morally obliged to tick them off, convinced that candid disclosure constitutes the soundest diplomacy.

The public character—a familiar to an unspecified number within and outside his academic habitat: tradespeople, medical doctors, Democratic Party pols, policemen, poets, journalists, letter carriers, lawyers, editors, groundskeepers. He has reached the point where, as Goethe says, a person becomes historical to himself, and "his fellow human beings become historical to him." In the course of a relatively long life, the narrator, Daniel Aaron, materializes into a type of native son neither estranged from the collective American family nor unreservedly clasped to its bosom.

When I was growing up, the word *American* was an antonym of the word *foreign.* Everyone knew, of course, that America was a "nation of immigrants" and that all Americans should be proud of their respective ancestries, but by adolescence I had run into people who made invidious distinctions between earlier and later arrivals to the United States and between their countries of origin, which is to say that if you were white and middle class and Protestant or the right kind of Roman Catholic and if your family had been living in America for a long time, you were more likely to "fit in" with less friction than did poor people of vague ancestry with dark skin and funny accents.

Over the years, I learned quite a lot about the imperfect workings of the "melting pot." Clearly it took longer for immigrants from exotic places to shed their foreign markings and to dissolve into their new homes than it took immigrants from Northern Europe, but no matter where they came from, new Americans weren't automatically treated as "family." The hyphen in Italo-American, Polish-American, Mexican-American, and so on drew the line between a qualified and a full acceptance. Theodore Roosevelt, with the German-Americans in mind, gave a special twist to the term *hyphenates* during World War I: he meant the foreign-born who retained old allegiances. Nathaniel Hawthorne was thinking "hyphenatically" in the 1850s (he was then American counsel in Liverpool) when he angrily expostulated, "I do hate a naturalized citizen; nobody has a right to our ideas, unless born to them."

Such sentiments were common before the age of correctness dawned. Ugly racial epithets (*nigger, kike, spic, greaser, chink, wop,* and the like) were still part of the vernacular. Only if you looked and talked and dressed like everyone else were you likely to escape contumely on the street and playground. These were the givens and to be expected. In my schoolboy days, it would never have occurred to me to challenge unwritten conventions; I modeled myself on my fellows. In adolescence, sensing that some of the boys I played with and competed against had arbitrary notions about who belonged and who did not, I grew more calculating. So far as I can tell, I suffered no permanent psychic bruises and was never barred from places where I wanted to be or from persons I wanted to meet. Just the same, there were moments when I felt myself to be an outsider disguised as an insider.

My early childhood was spent in relatively unchartered Los Angeles, and by my tenth year, both of my parents were dead. Two years later, in 1924, I returned to my birthplace, Chicago, uneasy in what seemed to me now foreign surroundings, hedged between the "gentile" world at large and the Jewish microworld of kith and kin of which I had never felt a part. Thereafter, a long, slow, and haphazard exploration of America culminated in 1943 with a doctorate in Harvard's new program in the history of American civilization, which signalized my merger with the USA and my dehyphenation.

I was now lumped with what the Frenchman Crèvecoeur called (in 1782) "this promiscuous breed, that race now called American," and I was acting the role of licensed practitioner of American studies in the United States and elsewhere. But there was still something of the outside observer in my disposition, a felt affinity with Thorstein Veblen's "renegade Jew," one of "these aliens of the uneasy feet." Like Emerson, a guiding spirit, I was just as comfortable with cranks, prophets, dissenters, utopians, and nonconformists as I was with their conservative opposites. Temperamentally a watcher and recorder, I never tried or wanted to be "leader."

Scattered through *The Americanist* are backward glances at fourteen "presidentiads" (Whitman's coinage for presidential terms of office) that spanned my lifetime. These interpolations are too biased and fragmented to pass as "history" and say more about me than they do about occupants of the White House. Some of the comments and judgments herein, many of them drawn from old journal entries, lack historical dignity and weight, and not all of the "facts" cited here are certifiable. But they do record my feelings and opinions close to the moments I entertained them, so they can be said to have an apocryphal validity and serve as signposts for my dash through the twentieth century.

When I first became aware of them, presidents were majestic eminences but fashioned out of common clay. National myth assured us that anyone with the right stuff (girls excepted, of course) could rise to the highest office of the land. None of my friends ever confessed to me that he wanted to be president, and I remember being startled years later when the grandson of Chief Justice Charles Evans Hughes confided to me during a long car ride that he had always taken it for granted that he might be president one day. Of course I never gave Negroes or Jews any chance to be chief magistrate when I first began to consider such matters. Presidential elections recurred like national holidays and, for a long time, seemed of less moment to me than heavyweight title fights or the World Series. Only after the election of Franklin Delano Roosevelt in 1932 did I regard them as crucial contests that could well determine the future of the Republic. All the same, my friends and I always saw presidents as emblems of power and authority. Hence, we would challenge one another, "Who do you think you are, president of the United States?"

PART ONE

I

I was born in Chicago, August 4, 1912. Both of my parents were dead by my tenth year and virtual strangers to me before they died—my mother in 1921, in the Pottenger Sanitorium in Monrovia, California; my father a year later. Nor was I in rapport with relatives, friends, or other informants who might have been able to fill in the gaps of family history had I been curious enough or geographically close enough to consult them. The snippets they provided never coalesced into a consecutive story. But over the years, I did pick up a smattering of alleged facts about the short lives of Rose Weinstein (1883–1921) and Henry Jacob Aaron (1879–1922), both small children when they emigrated from their different Russian birthplaces to New York City. I never tried very hard to find out the circumstances that brought them, why and when the two families moved on to the Midwest, and what happened to them after they had settled in Chicago. The few scraps I picked up came from anecdote and hearsay.

One story relates to my father's mother, who long outlived him. It seems that during one tough period, she preserved family dignity by a clever subterfuge: would-be dispensers of charity about to investigate reports of a hungry household were put off by the sight of scrubbed children in scrubbed rooms and by the smell of turnips cooking on the stove. Other reminiscences have to do with one of her grandfathers, who had lived in Baltimore for a time in the 1840s before he returned to his homeland, and with a second grandfather (or was it the same one?), who remembered the frozen corpses of French soldiers, their blue uniforms visible in the snow, on the road to Smolensk.

Grandma Aaron was my last link to a world that then seemed to me constricted by musty orthodoxies and totally incompatible with my secular America. A pious and time-weathered woman, she must have felt responsible for the religious grooming of her eldest son's parentless kids. In her eyes, we had stopped being Jews even before the death of our parents, and she did what she could to retrieve us. It was too late in my case. I was like one of those New England children captured and "Indianized" during King Philip's War who refused repatriation and chose to remain with their captors. My unwillingness and inability to "come home" to what I considered to be a foreign place wounded her deeply and confirmed her worst fears. Even before I married a gentile, she considered me lost. Had she known that my future father-in-law would urge me to change my name before I married his daughter (to him all Jews were "rebaters" and dollar chasers), I doubt it would have surprised her.

I know even less about my mother's murky family history and her early years than I do about my father's. It was as if large segments of her life had been blotted or distorted by rumor or gossip. From the wispy recollections of her in-laws that came to me secondhand, she appears to have been more socially and intellectually unconventional than my father's people and more casual about religious observances. Apparently her opinions and style of living didn't sit well with the in-laws, who, while showering her with superlatives, remarked sotto voce on her extravagance and impulsiveness, the very qualities that in retrospect drew me to her. I like to think that, like me, she envisioned an America that incorporated and superseded the older civilizations from which it derived. In any event, I play with the fancy that one important event in her life foreshadowed my introduction to American history.

That event was the sinking of the British liner *Lusitania* by a German submarine on May 7, 1915, a few months before my third birthday. Among the notable nonsurvivors aboard the torpedoed ship were the homespun inspirational journalist Elbert Hubbard and his wife, Alice, revered names in our household. A decade before, my mother had been a member of Hubbard's Roycroft Community in East Aurora, New York, and I and my brothers and sisters grew up in the aura of its founder, "Fra Elbertus," the sage. His strenuous apothegms and preachments echo dimly in my family history. The story has it (for everything I know about those days is second- or thirdhand) that Elbert Hubbard treated my mother as a surrogate daughter. His fatherly admonishments to "Sun-up" are inscribed in her leather-bound autograph album along with other affectionate expressions of esteem from fellow Roycrofters and from such illustrious visitors as Clara Barton and the poet Richard Le Gallienne, who testified to her "glorious womanly nature and magnificent soul." Hubbard's compliments were no less warm. She was his "Whitman girl," his "valued helper," the maker of "beautiful music," the beneficiary of his "love and blessings."

I have no idea when or where she met him (my guess would be at Jane Addams's Hull-House in Chicago) or by what steps she got to East Aurora. Nor can I reconcile my mother's patron with the inspired author of *A Message to Garcia* (1899), that tub-thumping tract against sloth and incompetence inspired by an incident in the Spanish-American War and distributed in the millions by governments and industries around the world. As Hubbard tells it, President McKinley, after many failures, at last finds the right man to deliver an important message to the commander of the Cuban insurgents, General Garcia. The young officer doesn't waste the president's time by asking a lot of fool questions. Dumped on the Cuban coast, he cuts through jungles, climbs mountains, and evades Spanish troops. Four weeks later, he locates Garcia. Hubbard's *Message* became a kind of media event and brought him international fame. By the time I read it, serious social historians had written him off as an inspired quack and huckster.

To label Hubbard a snake oil salesman, however, should not discount his importance as a guide for the culturally insecure. He had more than a touch of Benjamin Franklin's and Phineas T. Barnum's sly impudence and, like them, used it to deflate his patronizers. The audience he attracted and delighted consisted largely of outsiders like himself, the intellectually alert and mildly nonconformist people of moderate means, the self-educated graduates of Hubbard's alma mater, the university of hard knocks. My private Elbert Hubbard is still a shadowy composite of secondhand stories and fuzzy recollections, not the brassy public relations pioneer but the friendly bookish man who invited my mother to join him and the other Roycrofters at work and play. Something of that community's period charm and high-minded Victorianism emanates from the autographs and messages in my mother's album and from the volumes in our library signed by Fra Elbertus himself.

My mother appears to me in flashes. She returns me to the classroom from which I fled on the first day of primary school at a loss about what to do after the teacher sent me to the principal's office with a message. She reads to me and my siblings a story about a family who lived in a tree house with their dog, Brave Horatius. She's the haggard woman in a dressing gown who storms into the sleeping porch where my two brothers and I are engaged in noisy acrobatics. She's the person lying on a hospital bed in a cottage we are not permitted to enter (we stand outside and talk through the screened window).

My father seems hardly less remote, although I saw him constantly during our California years. He comes to life in his photographs, a strong man looking directly into the camera. He was the oldest of his widowed mother's four sons and served, for both good and ill, as family head. He studied law at a Chicago law school and, in 1899, set up his own firm in the Loop with his brother Charles as his junior partner. Family lore has it that his first important clients were meatpackers, but it now seems unlikely that they were part of the notorious Beef Trust, as I once believed. About 1915, when I was three, he showed symptoms of multiple sclerosis, and from its onset (so one of his brothers told me years later), he began to vent opinions on social questions that disturbed his conservative clients.

I have only a faint image of an invalid whose cheek I dutifully kissed at bedtime and whom, in my nightly prayer, I asked God to bless and to make well. The only words I can remember him saying to me are "Don't get gay, young man," but I can't forget his terrible sobs the evening that Miss Carl, his nurse and a Christian Science practitioner, gathered us around his wheelchair and announced, "Your mother has closed her eyes for the last time." We recited the Twenty-third Psalm. I didn't cry then, perhaps too alarmed about my eight-year-old self and the imminent future to think about him. A half century later, I read my mother's last letters to him, which were loving, uncomplaining, spirited, confident. Only then did I begin to understand the intensity of their devotion to each other and his feeling of loss and loneliness after she died.

In these last letters, she urges her crippled "dearest and best beloved" to dictate letters to his mother and to his brother Charlie (still in his twenties and soon to become my legal guardian), as it would please her if he did. She writes, "I think of you always and pray for you always and love you always with my whole heart." She adds that she knows he is surrounded by a charming "harem" (his nurses); she takes "great joy in signing myself your one and only *Wife*." How lucky we are, she tells him, to have had "fifteen years of love and faith and understanding, and mutual happy experience." She concludes: "And now with our darling children gathered about us, with a host of friends surrounding us, we can look back upon our blessings and from the depths of our hearts thank God. We have crowded the joy and happiness of thrice fifteen years into our married life, and joyfully, hand in hand, let us look to the future."

II

At some point in 1917, my mother and father left Chicago for Los Angeles with their five children. I remember very little of the three nights and four days en route, only the excitement of climbing in and out of upper Pullman berths and the vision of the male passengers of various sizes and shapes filing into the washing compartments at the end of each car: their unhitched suspenders dangle behind their backs; they carry leather toilet kits; I can hear the sounds of razors being stropped and smell the soap and witch hazel. I can also see the blanketed "Indians" on the railroad platform in Albuquerque and the stewards (white) and the waiters (black) in the dining car. It would be the last time our family traveled intact.

In Los Angeles we settled first into what extant photographs show to have been a square smallish house stippled with stones and then, in the next year, into a larger house on Mariposa Avenue, with a rose garden and fruit trees and a wisteria vine that all but covered the roof of the garage. In this haven for invalids, my father must have seemed a prime example of the "unhappy sick" coming west to be healed. I wasn't aware of the campaign then under way to keep the city from becoming a refuge for the ill or impoverished. We didn't fit the latter category, but I was instructed to reply to anyone who asked about my father's condition that he was recovering from a "nervous breakdown."

West coast sunshine seemed to do him good, and for a time he looked relaxed and comfortable. Several years later, as his disease took over, he required around-the-clock care. A bedroom and bath and a good-sized reading room (we called it the "library") were added to the first floor, and it was there that I headed the morning after he died, possibly to escape the buzz of adult voices and possibly to dull guilt pangs. A few days before, I had nagged to go to a neighborhood party on the Fourth of July, which also happened to be my father's birthday, and I made a nuisance of myself by getting sick. His death marked the end of an idyll and the beginning of a period of dislocations and adjustments for me and my brothers and sisters.

What I've chosen to remember about those days aren't my father's medical tribulations or the flu my brother David and I contracted in the 1919 epidemic but the house on Mariposa, our never-to-be-duplicated style of living (a big car and a chauffeur to go with it; maids; nurses, male and female), and an unlikely melange of objects and faces. There were rose bushes and Japanese gardeners; fruit trees (orange, lemon, peach); a waxy white avocado blossom; dead-ripe figs picked early in the morning, chilled in the ice box, eaten at breakfast with cream; an enormous toad nudging a calla lily in a dank recessed windowsill. I recall a conical straw sombrero; a stretch of lawn terraced to the sidewalk where an Airedale named Souvenir bit my thigh; a downstairs bathroom where somebody washed my mouth with soap for calling my sister a "bad name." I remember a "cannibal club" from the "South Seas," a gift to me from "explorer" and documentary filmmaker Martin Johnson, traces of blood easily discernible to me on its bulbous head; a Persian dagger "from the court of the shah," the cotton inside its sheath stained with "blood"; an "Indian club" (a pointed stick with a horse's tail attached to one end and a rock sewn in buckskin attached to the other); a bust of Queen Nefertiti; a portrait of Beatrice D'Este; Abbey's Galahad, pure and pensive, standing beside his charger; two large oil paintings of a churning California surf; a Steinway piano.

To the smart urbanites of the eastern seaboard, Los Angeles in the early 1920s was an overgrown country town of hicks and Yahoos from mid-America, a kind of traffic-ridden rabbit warren on the Pacific. My Los Angeles was a low-keyed paradise spiced with hazards. I often stayed outside from morning to dusk. In the neighborhood's plethora of empty lots, my companions and I built forts, dug trenches, and staged battles with mud slingers (spring wands tipped with clumps of clay), homemade slingshots, and, on occasion, BB guns. I survived these skirmishes without losing an eye, had my share of memorable fistfights, and joined the Daredevil Club. To qualify for the club, you had to slide down the guy wire of a telephone pole, jump from one garage roof to another, hang on the edge, and then drop to the ground. To break into the yards of the Pacific Electric Railway, snitch explosive caps from sheds, and place them on the tracks was to transform a naughty boy into a train-stopping saboteur; and to be chased by the police and to reach home unscathed and uncaught was exhilarating and scary.

My criminal career technically began and ended with a botched attempt to steal a large stick of gum when I was six years old. My companions, all consummate swipers, lifted big items like Hershey bars, whereas I was immediately nabbed by the store owner and threatened into honesty. Thereafter I was never tempted to steal—except once. Six years later, in Chicago's Jackson Park, I went off with a faded blue sweatshirt that had a gold galleon in full sail emblazoned on its back. I found it on the bottom of a rowboat and left a new suede jacket in its place. So the transaction was less a theft than an exchange.

Los Angeles was alive with construction when we arrived there. Small houses and bungalows mushroomed in assorted but predictable styles—Spanish and "Mediterranean" mainly, but all betraying evidence of architectural miscegenation. Although legends of their flimsiness were proverbial (they looked as if they had been hastily slapped together), they were sturdy or elastic enough to withstand the earthquakes that jolted the city. For my friends and me, these pullulating houses were places to rummage in after the carpenters had left for the day and to savor the smells of green lumber, resin, rolls of tar paper, kegs of nails, sawdust, and laths.

Los Angeles was a manageable city, easy to walk and bike in or to crisscross on the fat yellow streetcars, with nothing more dangerous to face than our own violence or the air assaults of red-winged blackbirds at nesting time. Patches of wooden oil derricks were nearby. So were Griffith and Westlake parks and Chutes field, home of the Los Angeles Angels, where, at the end of the games we attended, we would race through the empty stands and ransack every Cracker Jack box in search of baseball cards of Pacific Coast League players. I collected hundreds of these PCL cards and rarer cards of big-league stars that dated back to the early and late teens. Larger and of better quality, they featured such immortals as Honus Wagner, Ty Cobb, Christy Matthewson, Eddie Collins, Tris Speaker, Jimmy Archer, George Sisler, and "Three-Finger" Brown—a treasure trove irretrievably lost. They passed into my imaginary world with the Greeks and the Trojans, King Arthur's knights, and Indian chiefs.

Images and names of baseball players linger longer than those of my teachers, mostly women, at the Cahuenga and Alta Loma grammar schools, yet scenes and episodes beyond the confines of the classrooms but still within the precincts of the school remain vivid. They have largely to do with the tribal rights of a boy society that operated without adult supervision. Take, for example, the Bulgers club, an organization of obscure origins, easy to join but hard to get out of. Every morning, on spotting another member on the playground, you were required to shout "Bulgers" or get "corked" on the shoulder. It was perfectly legal for a member to approach you from behind and hit you with his fists before you could see him, and since I was absentminded to a dangerous degree, I decided, out of desperation, to resign. To do that, however, one had to "show blood." In my case, that meant walking to the handball court with an escort of fellow members, slicing my finger with a pocketknife until the blood flowed (a pin prick wouldn't do), and holding it up for group inspection.

My mates had little truck with kids of alien races and nationalities, but an exception was the school pet, a little boy affectionately dubbed "Snowball," whose parents had come to Los Angeles before the African-American westward trek. The only black in the school, he might have been cast in one of those *Our Gang* comedies where cute colored urchins and freckled towheads fraternized. That option wasn't open to many of the Asian and Mexican kids. All Hispanics, "greasers" in the racist Westerns of the Zane Grey school and in vernacular discourse, were well known to be treacherous and cowardly backstabbers. They invaded "nice" districts on Halloween and smacked the Anglos with soot bags. "Japs," though less threatening, weren't to be trusted either. You could never tell what was going on behind those oriental masks. "Chinamen," peddlers of fruit and vegetables, when not killing each other in tong wars, were cheerful and docile. I and my friends competed against Asian children in track meets for first-, second-, and third-place ribbons, but we stuck to the code of the tribe: those outside our space might have been living on the moon.

For that matter, I had little to do with any schoolmate who didn't live in a house like mine or read books or eat the same kinds of food. One exception—his name was Homer—invited me into his mother's kitchen for an afternoon snack. She cut us thick slices of spongy white bread heavily doused with sugar. I had never eaten such fare and thought it outlandish. Like most boys my age, I was a conformist on matters of food and dress and suspicious of innovations imposed by elders. By the time I was ten, I fit comfortably in the standardized America Sinclair Lewis sketched in *Babbitt* (1922), although I couldn't find much of my Los Angeles in his uniformitarian Zenith when I read the novel a decade later. I had only to review the photographs and newsreels of the 1920s to spot variety in the uniformity, even in some of the machine products that at first glance looked alike.

Take cars, for example. All cars are cousins, but if you paid attention to hoods, fenders, headlights, and hubcaps and to their distinctive tilts and tones, you learned how to appreciate their striking differences. The 1917 Cadillac touring car my father exchanged two years later for a 1919 model had had big tires prone to punctures and blowouts, canvas curtains with sewn-in isinglass windows, and jump seats behind the driver. From a distance, it looked like a Peerless, but when you got close enough, you could see that it lacked the Peerless's telltale signature: the semicircular lines of metal grafted on the back. The evocative names of cars came trippingly off the tongue: Auburn, Stutz, Packard, Hudson, Daniels, Reo, Hubmoble, Marmon, Overland, Franklin, Paige, Winton, Jordan, McFarland, Kissel, Maxwell, Stanley Steamer. I contrasted the bread-and-butter familiars (Ford, Chevrolet, Studebaker, Dodge, Plymouth) with the enchanting exotics—the Dusenbergs festooned with crawling aluminum coils and the arrogant Issota Fraschinis—and with the kinds of racing cars driven by the film star Wallace Reid in such movies as *Double Speed* and *Excuse My Dust.* Cars were more than machines. Their owners gave them nicknames, pampered them, and grieved over their broken axles and smashed rear ends.

Similarly, the paraphernalia of golf was not standardized then to the extent it is today. My father's clubs gathering dust in the coatroom bore not numbers, as they do now, but names: niblick, driver, brassie, mashie, cleek, midiron. Golf tolerated a degree of individuality observable in the costumes worn by players as diverse as withered John D. Rockefeller, William Howard Taft (his knickers emphasizing his rotundity), and the internationally renowned Bobby Jones.

Such bits of Americana are still haphazardly registered in my historical calendar. It opens with the *Lusitania* incident and continues through World War I (the first great event of my life) to November 11, 1918, one week after the false armistice we prematurely celebrated by running through the backyards of our neighbors beating pots and pans. I was then six years old. I wore an aviator's overseas cap (one of my uncles was in the Air Corps) and a sailor suit. I owned a small arsenal of toy guns, bought thrift stamps, acted out such prescribed rituals as chanting "Step on a crack" while walking on sidewalks: "Step on a crack, break your mother's back" was accompanied by careful leaps to avoid that catastrophe, while "Step on a crack, break the Kaiser's back" was accompanied by determined stamping. I associate the war with the taste of potato bread and with two soldiers, convalescing from a gas attack, who taught us such songs as "Pull Your Shades

Down, Mary Ann," "Good Morning, Mr. Zip, Zip, Zip," and the one that ended with the mournful refrain "You can always find a little sunshine in the YMCA."

I read about the war in my brother David's Boy Allies series and in such books as *With Joffre on the Battle Line*, but war photography and propaganda films made a stronger impact. D. W. Griffith's *Hearts of the World* (1918) and a grisly film entitled *Behind the Door* (1919) were especially memorable. In the former, "Huns" wearing spiked helmets brutalized two nice French girls. (Given the "Boche" partiality for saw bayonets—so significantly different from the needle-shaped ones preferred by the French— and their inhumane treatment of nuns, whom they used as bell clappers, this was hardly surprising.) In *Behind the Door*, a story of revenge, the details of which are a little cloudy after eight decades, a U-boat captain shoots the wife of an American naval officer out of a torpedo tube, after which her husband captures the German officer and extracts a terrible retribution: he skins him alive. The procedure was preformed offscreen (hence the title of the film), and the last shot, I seem to remember, was a smear of something shocking.

Some of these films, including Charlie Chaplin's war parody *Shoulder Arms* (1918), were projected against a large window shade in our living room, which lends credence to my father's purported "interests" in the movie business. No one ever spelled out for me what these interests may have been, and I didn't ask, yet the memorabilia of moviedom in our house, the actors we saw and occasionally met, suggest more than a casual connection between my father and the film people.

One link may have been Mr. Will Connery, inheritor of a Chicago coal fortune and much attached to my ailing parents, especially my mother. He drove a rakish Locomobile painted battleship gray and once took me to Vernon to watch a prizefight. Now a part of Greater Los Angeles, Vernon was then a rough factory town where the sporting crowd came to drink and gamble and to take in the four-round "exhibition" bouts (state law banned prizefighting). We were joined in a smoke-filled ramshackle arena by two of Mr. Connery's friends, H. C. Witwer, a thin sharp-faced man whose popular magazine series *The Leather Pushers* was being filmed, and Jim Jefferies, the U.S. heavyweight champion until Jack Johnson knocked him out. During one of the bouts, a woman held up her swaddled infant and screamed at one of the boxers, "My baby can lick you."

Another link between my family and the movies was the Japanese actor Sessue Hayakawa and his wife, Tsuru Aoki, friends of my parents. A huge batch of Hayakawa's mail from all over the world was stashed in a wooden chest in the hallway of our house, waiting his return. Postage stamps from these letters started my first stamp collection. He headed his own production company and played "Asian" characters in films that appealed to a broad international audience. The Hayakawas left California the year before we did and vanished from my scope until Sessue's emergence as the fanatical Japanese officer in *The Bridge over the River Kwai*. In 1973, I hoped to look him up on my first visit to Japan and to ask him about the Los Angeles days, but he died shortly before I got there.

Movies were still being shot on the streets in my Los Angeles, and film stars weren't fixed in the firmament; they often came down to earth and mingled with mortals. Tom Mix, wearing his white sombrero, waved to me on my tenth birthday as I and my friends were en route to watch Douglas Fairbanks in *Robin Hood*. A tipsy Mabel Norman rang the bell of our rented beach house between Venice and Playa del Rey and asked to use our telephone. Mr. Albert Christie of Christie Comedies promised to put me into one of his picture shows if I acquired one more freckle. Alice Joyce and her then husband Tom Moore lived across the board-walk from us; one night she materialized as a blond fairy queen, shimmery in sequins, and paused to say good night to her pretty daughter before taking off grandly. Mack Sennett occupied a large establishment nearby. I watched his black cook truss up and decapitate a large white goose and was much impressed by the geyser of blood.

Thanks to a neighborhood friend, whose father, a Warner Brothers executive, had "discovered" Rin Tin Tin, I was able to get into the studio and see the famous German shepherd hurl himself at the wire enclosure. I was one of the bunch of kids brought in to play with a bored Jackie Coogan, two years my senior. At the premiere of *The Covered Wagon,* I watched the searchlights sweep the skies over Grauman's Egyptian Theater; limousines deposited celebrities; and heaps of Indians, imported from reservations, held powwows on the theater's flat roof and danced in warbonnets to beating drums. An elaborate stage prologue preceded the main event: on the screen, a train of tiny covered wagons off in the distance slowly wound its way down a mountain road until real wagons debouched from the wings onto the stage; there, performers in pioneer dress sang "O Susannah" and danced hoedowns, and the "Indians" bellowed war chants. Finally came the epic movie, in which there was something for everyone. Burning arrows ignited a circle of prairie schooners; old frontiersmen squirted tobacco juice; young fathers propped their rifles in between the spokes of wagon wheels and took aim at the circling "redskins" as mothers in poke bonnets clutched their children—or so I remember.

Other than a faded recollection of Grauman's Egyptian Theater, amusement parks at Venice and Ocean Park, and a pastiche of shops and gas stations, my architectural memories are few and tenuous. I remember a row of steps flanked by two stone lions that guarded the entrance to the house of Mary Pickford and Douglas Fairbanks; the Alexandria Hotel (I recall standing on a chair in a curtained dining room and observing in a loud voice that a woman at the next table was smoking); Huntington Hall in Pasadena, a boarding school my sister Judith attended until a dismissed groundskeeper shot his wife (or was it the principal?) and set the school on fire. I have sharper impressions of Pasadena's annual

Tournament of Roses, a tedious New Year's Day of flowering floats. Later I would think of Pasadena as a nest of itinerant scholars attracted to the great Huntington Library in next-door San Marino. On several of my scholarly forays, I stayed at Cal Tech's Athenaeum and socialized with visiting foreigners, such as A. L. Rowse of All Souls, the self-declared intimate of "Winnie" Churchill.

The Ambassador Hotel was under construction between 1919 and 1921. The section of Wilshire Boulevard west of it was a dirt road. I was ten years old when the hotel opened and close enough to it to monitor its evolution, to marvel at its lawns and gardens, and to gawk at the well-groomed beasts and riders about to perform for the hotel's guests. I have a distinct memory of a short stout man in a blue uniform, waiting for an elevator in the Ambassador's gleaming lobby. It was Marshall Ferdinand Foch, former commander in chief of the allied armies.

When we left Los Angeles in 1924, the city's building boom had slackened, and the great bull market of the decade was yet to take off. By this early stage of our orphanhood, we were out of the Mariposa house, and what remained of the "family" (my older sister and brother had already returned to Chicago) was housed in a small yellow duplex near Pico Boulevard. I asked Aunt Miriam, my father's youngest sister, in charge of our shrunken quarters, if we were now "poor." We had to economize, she said, but I don't remember feeling deprived of anything that mattered. Two years later, we boarded the Union Pacific for the East, heading to my birthplace, Chicago.

Woodrow Wilson, elected president three months before I was born, died in February 1924, just before my dismantled family returned to Chicago from Los Angeles. By then, he was a name and a fading face. I took for granted what my elders said about him, that he was a "good" president martyred by a cabal of "willful men" bent on torpedoing his League of Nations. That image changed as I began to see him and World War I through the eyes of his disenchanted critics. Wilson, the noble "progressive" of his administration, had capitulated to the war spirit and yielded to the economic and political pressures he had once bravely resisted.

The picture of a prissy, tight-assed, racist Presbyterian was rife in the journalism and literature I was reading in the 1930s. The most persuasive sappers of Wilson's reputation—among them H. L. Mencken, Randolph Bourne, John Dos Passos, Edmund Wilson, and E. E. Cummings—thought him unctuous and hypocritical, a carrier of the Victorian virus they abominated (and suppressed) in themselves. To be sure, his Republican enemies were also abominable, but that didn't excuse his readiness to suspend civil liberties in wartime America, his prim vindictiveness (keeping Gene Debs in prison, for God's sake), or his Jim Crow sympathies. I learned to scoff at Wilsonian rhetoric that salved his Mexican intervention; I read exposés of his ulterior design to open up foreign markets to U.S. penetration.

Wilson was among the best-educated U.S. presidents, a fluent speaker and writer, an academic man—pluses for me at one time. I was lulled by his sonorous prose and "progressive" sentiments— closer to mine, I thought then, than those of his virulent opponent Theodore Roosevelt. Yet he never kindled in me more than the dutiful interest one was expected to show toward major public figures, especially those who had been "misunderstood" or "betrayed." In time, I preferred crustier and lustier types, even the self-promoting egomaniac TR, and although Woodrow Wilson had long figured in family lore as the martyred president and a great American, I never looked behind the glinting rimless spectacles, the stiff collar, the silk hat.

Wilson was living in retirement when the presidential campaign in 1920 reverberated in the playground of the Cahuenga grammar school. Democrat James M. Cox and Republican Warren Gamaliel Harding were simply political sounds. The hero we mindlessly cheered wasn't even a candidate, although he had sought the nomination. Challenged in the schoolyard and asked whom you were for, the correct answer was "Hoover." If you said "Cox," you got biffed. Harding materialized in the newsreels and in rotogravure sections of Los Angeles newspapers, a handsome silver-haired man dressed for the links, swinging golf clubs, getting on and off trains. Then he died all of a sudden and was reduced to a postage stamp in my album. I have only vague recollections of his trip to the Northwest, his lethal indigestion, the funeral train, and the unfeigned national grief before he was exposed and disgraced.

By 1935, he had pretty much turned into a symbol of a sleazy era, a scamp and a joke. One associated him with H. L. Mencken's famous description of "Gamalielese," the style of a "rhinocerous liberating himself by main strength from a lake of boiling molasses," and with E. E. Cummings's elegy on the man who could write a simple declarative sentence with seven grammatical errors. One hot New York summer night in 1955, Richard Hofstadter and I, working in his Upper West Side apartment on our American history textbook—both of us too tired to sleep—read aloud Harding's inaugural address and couldn't stop laughing. Rumors of the "tar brush" in his ancestry and disclosures of his furtive sexual adventures complemented the picture of the noble-looking clown who never wanted to be president and wouldn't have been had not corrupt wheeler-dealers made him their pawn. A few biographies of him years later made me wonder if he were the complete slob of his detractors or if his tormented administration was such a total disaster. I began to think of him as a character in a novel, like Hurstwood in Theodore Dreiser's *Sister Carrie*. The sad story of poor, unvindictive, bloviating Harding shrouded in the smoke from Teapot Dome adds a touch of poignancy to presidential history. He was dead long before I got a handle on him. ☙

III

Returning to Chicago at the age of twelve, discombobulated and a little fearful, was like moving to an alien planet, at least until the city commanded my limited loyalty and I could pretend to be at home in it. In time I learned to boast of its violence and exaggerate the exploits of its gangsters, the brutalities of its police, the number and variety of its fatalities, and the clownishness of its mayor William Hale ("Big Bill") Thompson, who had vowed to "biff" the king of England in the "snoot" if he ever dared to show up in the Windy City. I could not have shut my ears to the fanfare of the Loeb-Leopold murder trial (the victim of the accused lived only a few streets from our apartment) any more than I could have averted my eyes when the elevated trains in the Loop threaded blocks of tenements close enough for the passengers to catch the expressions on the faces of their occupants. I did, however, hold the city at a psychic distance. Chicago was an apartment house on Greenwood Avenue, the Charles Kozminsky grammar school (memories of which I have suppressed), and miles of anonymous streets. It was Jackson Park where relics of the World's Columbian Exposition were still extant, a place to come back to during the holidays to meet with relatives and ephemeral friends. It was oceanic Lake Michigan, a mere fifteen-minute walk away. It was a piece of the world I tentatively explored and marveled at, yet for reasons I can't explain, it remained alien territory. In years to come, I wrote about Chicago in literature at some length; in 1929 I left it with no regret.

For a long time, Uncle Charlie, the eldest of my father's three brothers and our supervisor and legal guardian, was a durable presence in my life, and his office at Clark and Dearborn was the power center of family governance. A settled bachelor when he took charge of our affairs, he was not prepared to play father to five children he scarcely knew. I could never think of him as a parent or feel completely at ease with him even when he was in a jolly mood and telling funny stories. Only when I grew older did I begin to have an inkling of the time and thought it must have cost him to be a guardian, not only to manage (and probably to augment) our modest estate, but also to make or withhold vital decisions. It can't be said that he "brought us up," for he had too many other and larger fish to fry, but he kept a concerned watch over our triumphs and fiascoes. I feared and resented his comments on my mediocre high school record, but his bluntness was curative, never mean or petty, and prompted by his high expectations. It was reassuring to be told that he didn't care what I did so long as I did it well, though his words could not dull the sting of his prediction (after hearing me perform in *The Pirates of Penzance*) that I was plainly destined to end up as a banana peddler. I dedicated my first book to him in 1951, with the mental addendum, "Take that!" Rereading his old letters to me, I was chagrined to find them avuncular, encouraging, and affectionate.

Uncle Charlie married soon after my grandmother died and lived until his middle nineties, satisfied, I think, that we had turned out as well as we did—even inclined on occasion to boast about us. He had had to put up with many alarms and adjudications during his tenure as guardian, but he had never tried to be a "dad," and I wasn't sorry about that: I had no wish to become a part of the well-to-do Jewish society to which he belonged. I separate Uncle Charlie from the all-purpose fathers I always seemed to be looking for to set me straight on matters of heart and mind, but he did what he could at critical moments to keep me from making an ass of myself.

Uncle Charlie supervised our affairs, domestic and financial, after the family retreat from Los Angeles. The reassembled household (five siblings; an elderly and absentminded chaperone, Miss Chandler from Coldwater, Michigan; and a string of cooks) shakily cohered for a few years. It fell apart as brothers and sisters veered off on their respective tracks—brother Benjamin to San Francisco to live with Aunt Miriam and her new husband; sister Ruth to the University of Wisconsin and, from there, to the University of Chicago Medical School; brother David to a spotty legal education, through mishaps and misadventures, and finally to a judgeship in the California courts; sister Judith, after a few discordant premarital attachments, to a durable and fruitful, if not rapturous, marriage.

Judith, the eldest, became the de facto steward of the Greenwood Avenue establishment after engineering the ouster of the ineffectual Miss Chandler, who liked to boast that her grandfather ("bless his old soul") had been an intimate of John Jacob Astor. When distracted, Miss Chandler would walk around the apartment in her underwear, proof positive to my sister that she was an immoral woman. Once empowered by Uncle Charlie, Judith took on the responsibility of hiring and firing, a touchy business awkwardly performed. In her last year at the University of Chicago and doing well in her studies, she paid scant attention to my own. How well I did in school didn't concern her much, but she set down a strict curfew—home by ten—while hosting mildly rowdy parties of her own. Her love affairs were frequent and tempestuous, each ending predictably in prolonged bouts of sobbing.

I recall the years from 1924 to 1929 in bits and pieces and totally without nostalgia. The best times were the intervals away from home, especially the weeks in northern Wisconsin, where, for two summers, I and five other boys took long canoe trips with a Cincinnati high school principal. Dr. Peasely, an ardent naturalist and woodsman, knew how to build a fire in a rainstorm and had a fondness for practical jokes. During his wanderings in upper Wisconsin, he had picked up a set of originals to whom we were introduced without foreknowledge. One of them, a storekeeper, shot out his big belly and knocked me into a heap of baskets. Another, Big George—an Ojibwa over seven feet tall—snatched my pup tent off the ground while I lay asleep, shook a club over me, and roared horribly. In the course of those two summers, we portaged over corduroy roads, shot rapids, and visited an Indian reservation in Lac de Flambeau. At the end of one long day, as I sat alone on a log and drank coffee and watched a theatrical sunset, I had the one epiphany of my life, a blissful fusion of body and spirit. It lasted five seconds.

In Chicago, omens of the Great Depression—urban decay, unpaid school teachers, street crime—were there to be seen and interpreted by the end of the decade, but not by this Daniel, who lacked the prophetic skill of his biblical namesake. Some months before "Black Thursday" (October 24, 1929), a thin, white-faced man jabbed me with a nickel-plated revolver as I was leaving our apartment en route to a neighborhood club. When I asked him to hold the two lightbulbs I was carrying while I dug out the coins in my pocket, he said he was going to blow me to pieces. For the first time in my life, I felt fear physiologically. It was as if a big bag of cement were pressing me to the ground. A few years later, two guys with knives leaped out of the dark and took my overcoat, hat, and octagonal Elgin watch.

These minirobberies kindled some gut terror, but they were also instructive. Called down to the police station after the first mugging to identify a suspect, I watched a plainclothes officer slam the suspect against a desk. That the officer had the wrong man didn't matter. The suspect was a "sonovabitch" who would "steal his grandmother's last crust of bread." The police never bothered to follow up the second robbery, for good reasons. My assailants had disappeared into the trackless Black Belt whose mysteriousness Saul Bellow would evoke in his story "Looking for Mr. Green." Some of my black classmates lived there, but aside from our encounters on basketball courts and baseball fields, I knew nothing of their lives. It would not have occurred to me that some day I might forge friendships with any of the black kids— Chuck Sheldon, Georgia McGlasker, Oriental Madison—who sat at desks adjoining mine in Hyde Park High School. A basketball game between Wendell Phillips High (predominantly black) and Hyde Park (still mostly white) touched off a riot in the gymnasium. In areas where the black population pressed against jittery white enclaves, I sensed the racial tensions but gave no thought to their causes. They were part of the climate. So far as I was concerned, Wendell Phillips could have been a Chicago politician. Not until my midtwenties would I begin to have friends and colleagues who happened to be African-Americans. Then, and for a long time afterward, I displayed an overwrought affability in their company, as if I were trying to make up for an ingrained insensitiveness to what Ralph Ellison would call their "invisibility." An almost total absence of fellowship with black Americans until my early thirties surely must have accounted in part for the space that even later in life separated me from my closest black friends. Was the absence of easy fellowship related in some way to Jewish and black self-hatred or to the impulse that moved some minority writers to break out of their own mental and physical enclosures into an open society?

Slowly Chicago's scope expanded for me. I explored Jackson Park, where remnants of the World Columbian Exposition of 1893 were still visible. I smelled the thick stink of the stockyards when the wind blew from the west, without knowing that they had been a part of my father's world when he was starting out and that his first important clients had been meatpackers. The checks of the Fort Dearborn National Bank bore the stamp of a steer's head. Properly, one of the songs we liked to sing began, "She promised she would meet me / When the clock struck seventeen / In the stockyards, one mile away from town / Where the pig's feet and pig's ears / And the good old Texas steers / They are selling them now for seventeen cents a pound."

I went to the slaughterhouse with Al Baugher, who also lived on Greenwood Avenue. We rode to Halstead Street on the streetcar and from there to the shambles where we watched the squealing hogs and bellowing steers being processed into meat products. Then we went to Baugher's basement to dissect a pig's heart and a cow's eye with his father's surgical instruments. I was already talking, for no particular reason, about being a doctor, encouraged by a young intern whose girlfriend lived next door, but I doubt if my part in the rites conducted in a cellar reeking of formaldehyde was prompted by genuine scientific curiosity. Then and later, however, hospitals and laboratories were agreeable to me, and I was grateful to my intern friend for introducing me to cadavers in the University of Chicago anatomy lab and for passing me off as a medical student at Cook County Hospital. In that vast repair shop for damaged bodies, I watched herds of patients wheeled into operating rooms and stood by the surgeons as they cut and stitched.

I don't recall very much—only shreds and patches—of Hyde Park High School, which I attended in the middle to late 1920s. I still can chart the streets I traversed to get there and can resee some of the landmarks I passed en route, such as Frank Lloyd Wright's Robie House on Kenwood Avenue, but teachers and classmates are largely blurred or forgotten. What sticks are a few ceremonial occasions or moments of stress—for example, the time I was designated by someone in authority to open the door of Amelia Earhart's car when the aviatrix pulled up in front of our school. I remember singing in productions of *The Pirates of Penzance* and *Trial by Jury*. I was knocked unconscious by a falling ladder (to the huge delight of the student audience) during a performance of *Androcles and the Lion*, in which I played the lion; I remember the consternation of the director and the agony of my humiliation. I seem to have blotted pretty much everything else connected with my unsupervised and unsystematic education in those indefinite years.

That I managed to slip through Hyde Park High School, once an exemplary institution, in three and a half years was proof of its declining standards. I did well enough in the courses I liked but not in courses that seemed to me hard or boring. My most stimulating moments were visits to Kroch's Bookstore on Michigan Boulevard, where, in lieu of an allowance, I was permitted to buy a book every week. For this transaction I consulted Mr. Solley, one of the senior staff. (I favored historical fiction mostly or books about exotic places, like Tibet, or about New Guinea headhunters.) At the end of my scrappy education, I could read no foreign language with any facility and remained an innumerate to boot. I graduated without distinction to the disappointment of Uncle Charlie, who looked in vain for any convincing signs of promise.

In June 1929, my Uncle Charlie took me to Washington as a graduation present. With the Great Crash still several months in the offing and the economy riding high, the trip was done in style. We traveled on the Baltimore and Ohio Capitol

Limited, deservedly reputed for its cuisine and for its affable waiters (collectively referred to in those days as "George"), and we stayed at the Mayflower Hotel. There, in front of a shiny cigar counter, my uncle introduced me to an Illinois senator, I presume a Democrat, who boomed out: "Why Charlie, why didn't you tell me you were bringing your nephew? I would have introduced him to the president."

That's the closest I ever got to Hoover, one of those public persons of no fixed abode, always hastening to foreign places to cope with natural or man-made disasters. He parted his hair in the middle and wore high Hooverish collars even when he went fishing. His face was thick and benign. By the mid-1920s, he had hardened into Mr. Republican, although, like Eisenhower of several presidencies beyond, he was courted by both parties. I took small interest in politics then and was neither impressed nor depressed when he rolled to power on the GOP juggernaut in 1928, although the ebullient Al Smith had been my uncle's candidate in that election. Then came the great stock market panic, and the engineer president turned into "hapless Hoover," victim of a political catastrophe he could neither comprehend nor forestall. I might have warmed up to him had I known that he sometimes swore and liked to relax with a drink. He lives for me in Walker Evans's 1931 photograph of a storefront window behind which is propped an idealized poster portrait of President Hoover looking like a rugged cherub. ❦

IV

In September 1929, a few months after my seventeenth birthday, I went off to the University of Michigan. A more likely choice for someone like me would have been the Experimental College at the University of Wisconsin, which had been recently organized and directed by the philosopher and educator Alexander Meiklejohn. I was urged to apply there by my sister Ruth, then an undergraduate at Madison, but I chose Michigan, because my sister

Judith's current boyfriend was an enthusiastic Michigan alumnus. Planted in Ann Arbor, I enrolled in a premedical program, for which I was wildly unprepared.

In fact, I was too young and too undisciplined to attend any university, much less to enroll in a premedical program. By the end of my freshman year, I had given up the idea of becoming a doctor, convinced by bald insinuations that I didn't have a mathematical mind and would be best advised to stay away from "practical" subjects. That seemed sensible. So after a lengthy exploration of nocturnal themes in legends and folklore, I began a richly adjectival epic that celebrated the triumph of evil. "The Demoniad," as I called it, was a set of sketches and tales, mannered and facetious, illustrating the evolution of satanic organisms from the simple to the complex. It ended with Moon, giant whore of Heaven, impregnated by Sun (fiery lust), whose germ cells engendered comets. In the climactic scene, planned but unwritten, trustful souls were to waft heavenward anticipating angelic welcome, then the cloudy curtains were to part. Gazing down over the hopeful host of souls was to be the beaming face of Satan.

A commonplace book records other facets of my extracurricular life and spiritual meanderings in Ann Arbor. It opens with one of Baudelaire's invocations to his muse ("Receive 'neath thy wing / This priest full of sin / All the heaven I desire / Is her kiss in Hell's fire") and is sprinkled with quotations from the writers I was sampling. These included standard English authors but also a good many exotics I had come across in the enthusiastic appreciations of James Gibbons Huneker, my guide and master. He called them (Nietzsche, Strindberg, Leopardi, Hauptman, Huysmans, France) "soul wreckers," an irresistible endorsement at a moment when I was circumspectly flouting conformity.

I had joined a fraternity as soon as I got to Ann Arbor. It seemed easier than finding space in a university dormitory, and for a while I enjoyed the camaraderie and the convenience of being effortlessly housed and fed. In a few years, however, I wanted to get out of what was in effect a segregated community hardly less class-oriented and snobbish than the fraternities closed to Jews. Jewish exclusiveness in the 1930s seems all the more ridiculous given that it abetted the very spirit of the ghetto it ostensibly opposed. How disgusting it was for some of the Jewish fraternity men to label less socially favored brethren "kikes" because of their accents or manners, when only a few generations at most separated the spawn of early and late arrivals. I looked for companionship outside of my fraternity circle and began to cultivate a bohemian set of friends, citizens of a larger republic.

Most helpful in leading me into new pastures was an English composition teacher, Eric Walter, who told me I was "word drunk" but tolerated my grandiosities. In his class, I heard the name of Henry James for the first time and read *The Waves* of Virginia Woolf; and it was he who saw to it that I met and sat next to W. B. Yeats at a departmental social gathering. (Yeats, I noted in my journal, had a slight paunch and wore blue socks. His brown bow tie was carelessly tied. His eyes were bluish gray and watery.) Yeats and I talked about Irish fairy stories, about Lady Gregory and her ceremonial rituals, and about *The Countess Cathleen,* but I was too distressed at the plight of the poet turned spectacle to remember the questions I had planned to put to him. Even so, I was pleased to be in an honors program at a university where one could hear the great Yeats chant his poems, the elegant T. S. Eliot lecture on the poetry of Edward Lear, and the critic I. A. Richards recite with gusto some poems of D. H. Lawrence.

I graduated in June 1933, close to the nadir of the Depression, which I, jobless, was about to confront. Frequent excursions to dilapidated Detroit had familiarized me with Depression scenery, but the landscape of car lots, soup kitchens, and grimy neighborhoods that I had viewed as a stage set from a dystopian movie now loomed as a prologue to the future. Not quite twenty-one, callow and narcissistic, and with no marketable skills, I had been exposed to "life" through whorehouses and trips across the Detroit River to Windsor, Ontario, where one could buy and smuggle home good whiskey without great risk.

In Chicago, the Century of Progress International Exposition was in full swing. The fair, spread along the lakefront between Twelfth and Thirty-fifth streets, had taken seven years to plan and build, and by the time it opened for business, the national economy had hit bottom. I went to the fair a number of times (it cost fifty cents to get in), and although there was plenty there to gawk at and ponder, I chiefly remember a blur of pavilions and futuristic gadgetry. I can recall, too, the weary, disabled, or just plain lazy fairgoers being hauled around in rickshaws by hefty football players from the local schools; the Harvard anthropologist who photographed my head and catechized me at his fact-gathering station; and the raunchy entertainment on the midway, where Sally Rand, in simulated nakedness, floated powdery white in a smoky-blue haze and waved feather fans.

That I'd never worked in an office or held a responsible job didn't stop me from seeking and (with a certain amount of pull) getting an interview at the City News Bureau of Chicago, said to provide the best training in America for neophyte reporters, even one ignorant of metropolitan Chicago and its variegated neighborhoods. On my initiation day at the bureau, the city was hot and smelly—the wind blowing from the west—and North Clark was crawling with people who slept in their clothes and had nothing to do. A black man scuffled along abreast of me. The collar of his stained World War I overcoat was fixed with a safety pin. He turned abruptly and thrust his hands into my face. They were webbed in a membrane of yellow skin and glazed with dirt.

The editor of the bureau wasted no time questioning my credentials. The tryout he assigned me was simply to go to the "Women's Court" somewhere in the bowels of the Loop (for me, unexplored country) and return with a story. After many queries and wrong turns, I located the building, the room, and the presiding judge—a spare elderly man who wanted to know what I was doing in his court. He seemed satisfied with my explanation and benevolently invited me to sit by his side as he addressed the day's batch of miserables. Sardonic, soft-spoken, avuncular, he meted out his judgments in a cruelly droll way and called the drunks and prostitutes by their Christian names.

Among the company waiting in the courtroom were a small, anxious man—a recent immigrant from Sweden—and his accuser, a resident of the apartment house in which he worked as a janitor. She charged that he had attacked her with a potato masher. Because the janitor looked small and defenseless and she was a hefty woman with a bulldog face, I took his side and slanted my story accordingly. How the court ruled I've forgotten, but the bureau editor said my story was well written and added my name to the list of some four hundred better qualified candidates also waiting for employment. I could not even feign disappointment. Besides, I learned shortly afterward that I had been accepted as a graduate student at Harvard University.

v

Chicago had always been a way station of sorts, a takeoff place for summer camps in northern Wisconsin and for trips elsewhere. I was never sorry to leave it, never eager to return. My "home" during my last two years at the University of Michigan was an apartment house on Fifty-seventh Street near the University of Chicago, where three sets of couples lived, one to a floor, with a scattering of their kin. I often camped there on vacations, and there I stored books, random bits of Americana (Bristol glass, Bennington ware, Currier and Ives prints), and a curley maple desk I had bought from my Ann Arbor landlady. What drew me to this poignant and feckless community was its grit and insouciance and its strenuous intellectuality. Two of the occupants were Dartmouth College graduates I had come to know well in Detroit, one a steelworker, the other a gifted student of the anthropologist A. R. Radcliffe-Brown. There was a fair amount of drinking and neighborly sleep-ins in accommodating beds. All of this fed fancies of community living unbugged by materialistic hankerings. The happy interlude closed with the breakup of three marriages and a suicide. By that time, my stored possessions had disappeared, and I was out of Chicago for good.

Late in the summer of 1933, I saw a poster advertising "limousine service" between Chicago and New York City, twenty-five dollars one way. I showed up a month later at a designated corner on Cottage Grove Avenue an hour before the 10 a.m. departure time. I was lugging Uncle Charlie's old Gladstone bag stuffed with clothes, a laundry bag of odds and ends, a portable typewriter, and a phonograph. Most of my cash I hid in rolled-up pairs of socks. At midafternoon a beat-up touring car pulled up to the curb. Three people occupied the backseat, and two others sat in the jump seats. My place was up front with the unshaven driver, who told me that his name was Rossovsky and that Barney Ross, the lightweight boxing champion, was his cousin.

During the trip, Barney Ross's cousin puzzled me and the passengers by halting in alleys and side streets for no discernible reason—that is, until we learned that his employers had no license to operate outside Illinois. Presumably they had warned him to be on the qui vive for cops. They were a tough outfit. In Cleveland, their henchmen threatened to beat us up unless we unlocked the car doors and allowed one more passenger to squeeze in next to me. Twenty-four hours later, we crept into New York, Rossovsky at the wheel all the way and dozing from time to time without quite falling asleep. By now we argonauts were intimate friends, our reserve eroded by the whiskey I bought in Cleveland and by our enforced proximity. We sang songs and opened up the way people do when they never expect to see each other again. The Serbian grocer nervously anticipated a reunion with a brother he hadn't laid eyes on in forty years; a small fiery Russian in an electric-blue suit prophesied his murder by gangsters; an elderly woman passenger told us that she was heading for Washington to report the lynching of an Indian on a Montana reservation; a self-styled "college girl" confessed her anxieties as she was about to enroll in an eastern school. A real writer would have stored away these revelations and sketched portraits of the speakers. I was too self-absorbed or excited to reflect on the crazy excursion from Chicago to New York City and from there to Cambridge, Massachusetts, but I was reminded of it during the next few months every time a five or ten dollar bill popped out of my cache of socks.

PART TWO

Harvard University had not been my first choice for graduate English studies, and I wouldn't have gone there had the University of London admitted me without time-consuming conditions. To my surprise and relief, Harvard did, despite my uneven grades and inadequate preparation.

It hadn't occurred to me that Ivy League English departments might be leery of graduate applicants deemed unlikely to "fit in" (namely, those who looked or talked in ways that set them apart from their fellows), until my department chairman tactfully set me straight. Jewish students aspiring to a higher degree in English language and literature, he advised me, were sometimes deflected into departments (German, chemistry, and sociology, for example) where names and accents and looks scarcely mattered. He and his colleagues, he assured me, were confident that I faced no problems on that score (which, given my name, I obviously did), and he urged me to press on with my plans. His words disconcerted me a little. I had taken it for granted that someone like me with adequate grades and enough money and self-assurance could pretty much study what and where he pleased.

That assumption turned out to be true in my case. Tuition at Harvard was four hundred dollars a term, quite a lot in the 1930s, but I was reasonably sure that my dwindling inheritance could pay for the degree. In those lean times, families of four were surviving on twelve dollars a week. A bottle of milk cost eleven cents; a loaf of bread, twelve cents; and two packages of Lucky Strikes at the A&P, twenty-six cents. You could buy a gallon of gin for less than four dollars. I considered myself pretty well off, as indeed I was compared to the scores of graduate students who lived in monastic dorms or, more precariously, in grungy rooming houses short on bathrooms. Unless affiliated in some way with the Freshman Union or one of the college houses, outsiders foraged for grub in the local eateries, where it cost fifty cents for an edible meal and a few dollars or less for a fairly decent one. During my first year, I lived more than comfortably in a Linnaean Street apartment with three second-year law students, also University of Michigan graduates. They revered and feared their notoriously rude teachers and regarded their academy as both a kind of purgatory and guarantor of better things to come. My friends in the graduate school had no such expectations and, if anything, were more marginal to Harvard College than the unfledged lawyers. Indeed, for many students, "acceptance" into Harvard meant only admission into the college proper, and it took a little time for strangers with bachelor degrees from the provinces to wise up and adjust to that salient fact.

Even the comparatively well fed and comfortably housed from trans–New England discovered that they weren't part of the intangible networks that constituted the "real" Harvard. First-year graduate students often remarked on the university's chilling indifference. Would we arouse the slightest concern or curiosity if we expired in the middle of Harvard Square? Would anyone even bother to turn us over to find out who we were? There were moments in the winter months when the spirits sank with the temperature. During Christmas recess in December 1933, the thermometer registered twenty degrees below zero for more than a week. I lived on baked beans while reviewing three-thousand-plus lines of *Beowulf* for a course taught by George Lyman Kittredge, an immensely learned white-bearded scholar who could stop traffic on Massachusetts Avenue simply by waving his cane. It was a lugubrious time. The wind blew down the streets of a scruffy Cambridge, and there was no way to muffle the sounds of church bells on the ghastly Sundays when the few cafeterias open for business in the morning further depressed the depressed and when Widener Library was closed all day.

Widener was Harvard's hub. It was also its rialto where academic business was transacted, an unfathomable resource, and a retreat for the bruised and the wounded. The library stacks were then closed to undergraduate traffic, and I came to regard them as my private reserve. Alcoves on the upper and lower levels housed special collections: shelves of books (some of them untouched for decades) and files of defunct periodicals. Here you could carry on exercises in bibliographical research, track down obscure references, make serendipitous discoveries, and legitimately waste time. Here you were treated as a participant, however minor, in a common enterprise; and here was the soul of the university that, for all the reputed nose-in-the-air exclusiveness, was the heterogeneous and heterodox "great Good Place."

My teachers were largely philologists and textual scholars, men of learning and industry. Their critics charged that they were steeped in the dregs of a nineteenth-century scholarship totally devoid of intellectual content and demanding neither reflection nor analysis. That didn't seem so to me, but true or not, by my second year, I knew very well that the English graduate program was certainly remote from the actualities of Franklin Delano Roosevelt's first hundred days as president—and so it remained. I didn't think it inappropriate to read Chaucer and Elizabethan poets when my fellow Americans were out of work, but in the next two years, the question of what and why I was studying seemed increasingly pertinent. Unable to resolve it, I broke out of the philological thicket into more luxuriant territory.

I was sharing an eight-dollar-a-week room on Trowbridge Street with a Wesleyan University graduate, John Finch, a clergyman's son, disciplined hedonist, poet, and amateur blacksmith. His friend and Wesleyan classmate Charles Olson lived nearby. Olson, a six-foot-six mailman's son from Gloucester north of

Boston, wore his suit jacket like a cloak and startled me when he said "shit" right out loud in a restaurant. The occasion was lunch in a Cambridge eatery with Charlie and the self-pitying, backbiting Edward Dahlberg (1900–1977), author of *Bottom Dogs* (1926), a novel that fascinated and nauseated D. H. Lawrence and defined the world of degraded (lumpen) proletarian. Dahlberg repelled me that day, because he (then a Communist, no less) scolded our waiter for serving him food he didn't like. In 1963, I reviewed *Because I Was Flesh,* his powerful and rancid memoir, which I very much admired. Six years later, he praised my "remarkable insights" and suggested that I be his biographer. We broke relations after his venomous attack on Edmund Wilson, who had done so much to promote him. Eventually I described Dahlberg as "a visionary on a muckheap whose imagination is at once cloacal and religious."

Finch, Olson, and a few other like-minded friends in our Trowbridge Street digs enthusiastically espoused the "new" in literature and the arts, as Ezra Pound had recommended. We played and puzzled over a tape of Bela Bartok's second-string quartet, then seldom heard in the United States. We hashed over murkier parts of Dostoyevsky's novels and seriously thought of producing Shakespeare's *Troilus and Cressida,* after the poet and Harvard lecturer Theodore Spencer agreed to direct it. The project fizzled because Finch and Olson, who agreed that I would make an adequate Thersites, couldn't agree on which one of them ought to play Troilus. We could and did concur, however, that the Boston performances of the Ballet Russe de Monte Carlo were quasi-religious events and that its principal dancers were divinities.

Writers outside the canon and usually untaught in English departments had a special cachet. We especially relished the comical and savage grotesques of Nathanael West, recently published, and chanted in unison snatches of James Joyce's "Work in Progress." Herman Melville's books were central, thanks largely to Olson, who was then at the start of his pioneer voyage through

Melville's watery world. E. E. Cummings, whose name had not yet hardened cutely into the lowercase, was our touchstone for literary irreverence, our profane Peter Pan. We memorized his poems about whores, flowers, children, and theatrical proletarians. His verse and drawings celebrating the American burlesque lured us to the Old Howard, Boston's storied theater and former Millerite temple, where such striptease artists as Ann Corio and Gypsy Rose Lee leisurely disrobed. To give our mild dissipations a scholarly cast, we would discuss lofty themes in low surroundings and catch echoes of Petronius in the scurrilous exchanges of the comedians. It was our response to the Harvard followers of Irving Babbitt and Paul Elmer More, upholders of moderation, decorum, and self-constraint. While these epigones spoke for their preceptors, we made pilgrimages from Harvard Square to Scollay Square to sop up the atmosphere of the Hotel Imperial, a haunt of sailors and the place where, in the welcoming song of the master of ceremonies, "old friends meet." The return to Cambridge past midnight on a streetcar loaded with the soused and the sick provided a stimulating panorama of the Hub's lower depths.

To say that we subordinated the social and political to the aesthetic is only partly true, for the times certainly affected our tastes and judgments, and yet revolutionary forms meant more to us than revolutionary messages. The criticism we favored, whether celebratory or analytic, was not primarily ideological. We jeered at the call for a "socially significant" literature and at the very idea of ranking writers, as Edmund Wilson put it, by their "readiness to subscribe to the mechanical slogans of this or that political fashion." We agreed with him that great literature, however "nondoctrinal," had always dealt with "the larger events of the world." Hence we delighted in Orson Welles's Mercury Theater production of *Julius Caesar,* which transferred Shakespeare's Rome to Mussolini's capitol and made the totalitarian pageantry of black shirts, jackboots, and brandished banners seem theatrically and ideologically appropriate. Equally bristling were Clifford Odets's

Group Theater plays, both the agitprop *Waiting for Lefty* and the sugarcoated Chekhovian *Awake and Sing.* We distinguished the acting and staging from the Communist Party heroics.

In the spring of 1935, at loggerheads with myself, I took the advice of my old teacher and guide Eric Walter and applied for a fellowship at the University of Michigan. A slot opened providentially, and I used that academic year in Ann Arbor to rethink my options. I taught English composition with misplaced confidence to three sections of students, a high percentage of whom would flunk out by the end of the year. Too terrified to do more than call the roll when I started out, I quickly acquired sufficient nerve to handle the "thought-provoking" essays in our assigned text and to pontificate on social issues I knew little or nothing about. My students swallowed everything I said except my warning about the insidious influence of Thomas Wolfe, their favorite author, whose novels lifted their spirits and inflated their prose.

Under the guidance of two senior professors, I also began a systematic reading of early American history, and I enrolled in an American literature course taught by Howard Mumford Jones, one of the last polymath professors. His learning was said to be encyclopedic. A lanky man with a resonant voice and a red mustache, Jones was a vintage liberal spawned in the Midwest of Eugene Debs, Vachel Lindsay, and Robert La Follette. Some of his poetry had appeared in Mencken's *Smart Set,* but primarily his scholarly publications in literature and cultural history, both European and American, made his national reputation. He spiked his lectures with allusions to forgotten or obscure figures— a geologist, say, or the author of a pathbreaking work on calcareous manures, or an overlooked political theorist or economist or marginal regional novelist whom the serious scholar neglected at his or her peril. Jones was drawn to sweeping subjects and given to writing books with the words *civilization* and *culture* in their titles. If neither intellectually nor stylistically brilliant, they were solidly put together, packed with information, and lucidly composed. He was an energetic man, gruff, droll, untranquil. When crossed by bigots of any camp, he swelled with wrath, ever the American Democrat breasting the winds of doctrine—a sometimes testy, but always honorable, patriot.

Jones's translation from Ann Arbor to Cambridge, Massachusetts, in the fall of 1936 triggered my own return to Harvard, which I believe he tacitly engineered. It coincided with Harvard's three-hundredth anniversary and, most important for me, with the inauguration of the university's program in the history of American civilization, which set the course of my academic and professional career. I was on hand when Jones received one of the sixty-two honorary degrees awarded to an international galaxy of scholars, and I watched him and other dignitaries parade in their academic finery and deliver their tercentenary lectures. I heard Carl Jung's talk on the mandala, after which Charlie Olson questioned him on the mandala figure in *Moby Dick* just as if Jung were a run-of-the-mill academic. I was dazzled by Charlie's intrepidity.

One day in early autumn, 1936, I saw President Franklin Delano Roosevelt plain. His open touring car was only a few yards away when it passed slowly on Massachusetts Avenue. He looked as he did in the newsreels, the head confidently cocked, the jutting jaw, the hard grin. Lots of Republicans hated Roosevelt's guts and resented his presence, and many old-line Democrats considered him weak and pliable. My Uncle Charlie, for one, much preferred Governor Alfred E. Smith, the "Happy Warrior," but changed his mind after watching the president fight through his first hundred days in office. I hadn't been politically engaged enough and, in any event, was too absorbed in my personal traumas to think much about Roosevelt's success and failures. By the mid-1930s, however, I counted myself as an irregular in the Roosevelt legion, left of his New Deal administration and unhappy with the government's refusal to sell arms to Republican Spain but unqualifiedly hostile to the president's enemies. He was my hero. When I saw him that day in Cambridge, my arms shot up as if some force had yanked them, and I roared a cheer.

The implacable Roosevelt haters of the next two decades constituted a lively mix of loony "fascists," right-wing publishers and their hirelings, radio pundits, outré clergymen, old-fashioned populists, angry businessmen, and vengeful congressmen. Like Thomas Jefferson, Andrew Jackson, and Bill Clinton, FDR infuriated a lot of people to the point of madness. More puzzling to me was the resentment against his New Deal (called by some his "Jew Deal"), which wasn't confined to any class, race, gender, or geographical region. I was unaware then of the Congress's and the State Department's reluctance to open the country to a flood of German-Jewish refugees lest their admission exacerbate the mounting anti-Semitism in the United States or of FDR's refusal to get involved in this touchy issue until it became politically feasible, indeed almost obligatory, to lower the barriers that shut out doomed petitioners.

The president I spontaneously cheered at Harvard was a banner, a force, a fixture—above all, a voice. That he collected postage stamps and fancied sailboats and fathered a family of philistines and couldn't match his cousin Theodore's intellectual vigor and appetite for cultural diversity (or his wife's, for that matter) signified little in the long run. This was the man who hung like a WPA poster in the national classroom between 1933 and 1945 and who, with all of his imperfections, was by my criteria gallant and great. You could concede much to his critics, if not to his paranoid detractors, and still rejoice in his triumphs. Most Americans didn't anticipate his quick disappearance, nor were they prepared for it. I know that I wasn't. Only later did I recall the transparency and deadly refinement of his face in his last photographs, as if he were already a half ghost about to fly out of history. His death, in April 1945, left a hole in my world that none of his successors would ever fill. ❧

II

The Harvard I had come back to after a hiatus in Ann Arbor looked and felt different to me, as if the intervening rumblings, national and international, had shaken it up a little and made it less chilly and granitic. Vestiges of the pre-Conant era were still plentiful, but the university seemed denuded of its moss. Mandarins who stalked the Widener corridors as late as 1933 were dead or dotty. My new appointment had made me technically an "officer" of the university; my shift from English literature and philology to American literature and history brought me close to subjects I had long avoided. I felt as if I were looking at my times, my country, and myself with a new pair of eyes.

In the mid-1930s, Harvard had its share of mavericks and eccentrics—more, I think, than Yale and Princeton did—and a solid corps of the superrich. But although a sizable number of its undergraduates had gone to eastern preparatory schools, more than half hailed from public schools in every section of the country. Kind clung to kind in this striated community, but class distinctions pretty much stopped in the classrooms. "Meatballs," a mean term applied to students whose looks, accents, manners, habits, or racial origins signaled "outsider," were no less part of Harvard College than the white-shoe types. No one was denied access to the Harvard arena.

The Widener Library steps provided a space for a continuous forum at which exponents of any persuasion could let out steam and where hecklers could heckle. What prompted the usually cheerful disturbances in this period of social agitation and high jinks? One couldn't be sure. Uncomprehendingly I watched laughing members of the Hasty Pudding Society, young Frank D. Roosevelt Jr. among them, break up a pacifist demonstration. I listened to student proclamations and calls for student action on a variety of domestic and foreign issues, few of which touched more than a small minority of the Harvard undergraduates.

Then, as now, Harvard was a stopover for people in the news. Campaigning for his father, James Roosevelt lamely conflated family history with stunning advances in the nation that his grandmother Sarah Delano had lived through. Gerald L. K. Smith, Huey Long's populist lieutenant, harangued a jeering audience in Sever Hall and threatened to return to Harvard with his wool-hat boys and clean up the joint. Folklorist and musicologist John A. Lomax brought Leadbelly (Huddie Ledbetter), fresh out of jail and still in his overalls, to Emerson Hall. Seated on a kitchen chair on top of a desk, a cracked cup filled with gin in easy reach, Leadbelly accompanied his plangent work songs and blues on a big twelve-string guitar. But the high moment for me was a rally for the Spanish Loyalists, an emotional university gathering featuring as speakers Louis Fischer, a left-wing journalist, and André Malraux, novelist and volunteer flyer for the Spanish government. Malraux, gaunt and hollow-eyed, wearing an unpressed uniform and chain-smoking throughout his remarks, looked as if he had just stepped out of one his novels. We cheered him.

A call from the Quincy Street office of the newly installed James Bryant Conant followed Harvard's announcement of an extracurricular program for undergraduates who wanted (or ought to have wanted) to be less ignorant of their country's history and institutions. Mr. Conant greeted me pleasantly. How kind of busy me to see him and what an immense favor I should be doing him if I consented to become the first "counsellor" in this experimental enterprise. He was at once genial and distant. One learned from such interviews how the good manners and cordiality of one's superiors can act as a hedge to intimacy.

The idea for the program and the money to fund it came from a conservative alumnus and had nothing to do, as I once believed, with Conant's notion that Harvard men lacked ideological ammunition to confute the casuistries of the Reds and the Nazis. My job, I gathered, would be to entice students to confer with me on any aspect of American culture they might like to explore and to discuss with them any books from the formidable list on American history and culture drawn up by the faculty. A few did come to my make-do office in the library of the Harvard Union, and a fair number of interested or merely curious clients dropped in to hear the team of speakers I inveigled to perform. Out of the past stepped "Copey" (Charles T. Copeland), Harvard's perdurable relic who had joined the English department nineteen years before I was born. Archibald MacLeish, then in the throes of returning poetry to "public speech," read passages from his long poem in which he reminded his listeners that their sires had been a tough people.

Two strikingly un–Ivy Leaguish and authentically "tough" visitors also addressed my group. One was Vermont-born Stewart H. Holbrook, a former ballplayer, lumberjack, and newspaper man who had settled in Oregon and there absorbed the lore of the logging camps and the forest industries of the Pacific Northwest. With boosts from H. L. Mencken and *New Yorker* magazine's Harold Ross, he had dug up the histories of the "lost Americans" who had lived extraordinary lives. Holbrook was a soft-spoken fellow built hard and square like a steel safe. Although never a recognizable drunk, he had evolved into a quart-a-day man until a doctor told him to quit drinking if he didn't want his wife to collect his insurance. So he quit—cold turkey. He had delirium tremens for over a month, but he never took another drink, although he kept plenty of whiskey in his pantry for guests like me. He was a vivid evoker. I treasure his description of a winter scene just outside Duluth on a snow-spangled night: the rising moon lights a solitary whorehouse, and tethered to a nearby flagpole is a captive wolf.

The other "tough" visitor to my group was Edwin A. Lahey, also a short guy from the "real world." He was the most talked about of the nine professional journalists who inaugurated Harvard's Nieman Fellowship program in the fall of 1938. He had covered the sit-down strikes in Michigan and Ohio for the *Chicago Daily News* and gave my group a racy and not unbiased account of the ferment on the labor front, in vintage front-page style. Terse, witty, sardonic, he was a favorite of Felix Frankfurter and of the other Harvard New Dealers on the Cambridge–Washington circuit. A new breed of college-educated journalists had already begun to supersede the tough wisecracking reporters mythologized on stage and screen. Lahey became my model for the American newspaperman, and he constantly played that role. I cultivated a colloquial line of chatter and switched from donnish Scotch whiskey to honest bourbon because he and the other Nieman fellows, who had come to Harvard for professional and cultural replenishment, made me feel uncomfortably academic.

In public, I took a bullish stand on the Harvard extracurricular program in American culture, but although I tried hard to heed the warning of a *Crimson* editorial not to be a "banana peel on the road to culture," I wondered how many of my students were likely to explore and reflect on their civilization. Those of them who joined me at the history table in the Harvard Union dining room on Quincy Street showed no marked interest, so far as I could tell, in America. Most of them were lonely fellows or oddballs who came in search of company or simply out of curiosity and were easily distinguishable from the preppies. They weren't well-rounded students, and they displayed their angles. One had a passion for snakes, another for Vilfredo Pareto; a third turned his room into a gambling casino. Remarkable among these free spirits was a besotted Wagnerite and storehouse of esoterica who later became a friend and collaborator of W. H. Auden. Although a Jew, he kept a portrait of Hitler on his shelf.

I can only guess what these mavericks thought of me, but many years later, one of them wrote to me that I had mattered to him. Emile F. A. De Antonio ("Dee" to his friends) was expelled from Harvard at the end of his second year, which he describes as "the best damn thing that ever happened to me." Thereafter, by his own account, he worked as a teacher, barge captain, translator of opera librettos, and artists' representative. Once, during World War II, he flushed the manuscript of his just-finished novel down the bomb bay of his plane. He finally found his niche as the director of such much-admired films as *Point of Order*, a documentary on the Army-McCarthy hearings, and *Millhouse: A White Comedy*, an unclinical autopsy of President Nixon. De Antonio's accomplishments are preserved in the files of the FBI, for whom, as he put it, he had become "the ultimate document . . . , a pile of papers." When he died in 1989, he had long lost interest in Harvard or me, but there was a time, he wanted me to know, when I had put him on the "humanist-materialist path." He'd never known if I had any party affiliation or was "just interested in political and social trends," but I was the only teacher at Harvard he liked, "because," he explained, "you were young, and fresh, and naïve and liked the things you talked about."

My journal entry of June 16, 1937, mentions the subsiding of my "hot radicalism." This was pure twaddle, because my "radicalism" was largely rhetorical. The entry does suggest, however, that my three-year immersion in American literature and history (subjects I had disdained in college) had made me an adherent of what I loosely called in my first book, *Men of Good Hope* (1951), the "Progressive tradition." I distrusted most leftist commentators and critics, because I became convinced, while preparing for my general examinations, that they didn't know beans about the real United States—its geography and climates, the stages of its economic and cultural development, and (not the least) the variety and centrality of its religious culture.

The last was an important discovery for me. In the early 1930s, Puritanism was tantamount to repression, and the Puritans were popularly equated with witch burning, book banning, prohibition, and blue laws. My Harvard teachers scotched these canards and exaggerations. I was glad to learn that Puritans drank spirits and never burned witches, even though they did press to death or hang a few of them and occasionally whipped fanatical Quakers. In the ambiance of the New Deal, it wasn't hard for me to read into the Election Day sermons of the seventeenth- and eighteenth-century New England clerics some faint anticipations of a social gospel, a reconciliation of private enterprise and public spirit, a corrective to piggish self-aggrandizement, and a call for personal discipline and a practical social ethic. Here was a platform for a kind of "necessitated freedom" (to use a phrase of Emerson's) and a social democracy I was trying to formulate. I didn't catch the

authoritarian ring in my neo-Puritan response or pay much attention to the social views (most of them conventionally liberal) of
my instructors in the American civilization program.

Kenneth Ballard Murdock, the first director of the Harvard
program, was one of a popular trio who taught the survey course
on American literature. The other two, Francis O. Matthiessen
and Perry Miller, were both from Illinois, although the former
was a Yale graduate. Murdock was Boston and Harvard incarnate,
master of Leverett House and presumed successor to President
Lowell until Murdock's affair with and eventual marriage to the
wife of a faculty member cleared the way for his friend Conant.
Tall and courtly and delivering his lectures with a lofty, yet casual,
air, Murdock appeared to me extraterrestrial. I'd never met anyone so grand. His younger colleagues in English 7, the American
literature survey course, treated him unceremoniously, but I could
never address him with the informality he invited, nor, for a long
time, could I bring myself to call him by his Christian name. We
stayed friends, and he continued to do me quiet favors, but he was
warmer in his lectures than in the flesh and constitutionally Brah-
minical. After his second marriage, he seemed to diminish, losing
something of his authority and impressiveness.

His younger colleague and intimate Matthiessen lectured haltingly, as if he were minting his ideas as he spoke. Politically he was
to the left of Murdock and Miller—less historically oriented, perhaps, than either, but a subtler and more sophisticated literary
critic. Until undone by history, politics, and personal disasters, he
lived relatively secure and content inside his Pinckney Street bastion on Boston's Beacon Hill, amid piles of books and literary
quarterlies. Powerful associations (for example, with Yale's secret
society Skull and Bones) shielded him from the batterings inflicted
on less well-connected Harvard deviants. But then, in quick succession, came a series of unsettling events, personal and public, that
Matthiessen couldn't cope with. Russell Cheney, Matthiessen's
longtime companion, died, and the Harvard Matthiessen had vir-
tually grown into before World War II came under the manage-

ment of what he called "Conant's relentlessly mechanical slide-rule autocracy." The defeat of Henry Wallace in the 1948 presidential election (the only candidate, Matthiessen reminded me, who had read William James) and the Communist coup in Czechoslovakia (Matthiessen had banked on a neutralist zone between the Soviet and U.S. imperialisms) deeply depressed Matthiessen. So did his struggle to complete his book on Theodore Dreiser, which he didn't think had turned out very well. He committed suicide in April 1950, a year before its publication.

Matthiessen's slightly junior colleague Perry Miller added a Chicago flavor to the joint American literature survey course for which I did the donkeywork. Genial and attractive, he was the most boyish and flamboyant of the troika. He growled and grimaced and made broad jokes over the podium and alluded to his picaresque adventures in exotic places, but he was a pertinacious scholar and a demanding teacher. Graduate students had good reason to fear his explosions. (To the amusement of our friends, John Finch and I would dramatize the catechisms of the unprepared.) Perry Miller was my Dutch uncle—and I was his boy—until our rupture some years after I'd left Harvard for Smith College. This break in relations was provoked by my less-than-enthusiastic review of what Miller expected to be his most popular book and by our disagreement over the merits of Edmund Wilson, whom Miller had abruptly turned against. World War II both energized and undid Miller. He entered it in some noncombatant role and returned from it a romantic swashbuckler boasting about the Germans he had slain. After the war, Miller became an alcoholic, was ejected by his wife, and courted pretty graduate students. In a sense, he might be counted a war casualty.

III

My last three years at Harvard paralleled the decline and fall of the Spanish Republic. They ended just before the signing of the

German-Russian nonaggression pact in August 1939 turned the world upside down and disenthralled those of us who may have disagreed on many political and social issues but who never conceived the possibility of a Hitler-Stalin rapprochement. Although under attack from many quarters because of the preposterous treason trials in the USSR and rumors of Soviet thuggeries in Spain, the American Communist Party still enjoyed the support of the "progressive camp." The few acknowledged Communists I knew hardly bothered to hide their party affiliation. My office mate Robert Gorham Davis casually alluded to meetings of his Harvard cell, but they seemed to matter less to him than the daily bets he placed on the horses from his Warren House phone. His party activities (he wrote pseudonymously under the name of an ancestor, Obed Brooks) were strictly extracurricular. I doubt if his students—including Norman Mailer, an intense hungry-looking fellow—knew or cared about his politics.

My friends and I considered ourselves a part of the United Front, by no means walkers of the Communist Party "line" but unquivocally antifascist. It never occurred to me to join the Communist Party, which despite all its efforts to Americanize itself, still seemed "foreign" and "alien" and even comical. But I was eager to learn more about Marxism and its classical texts. An opportunity to do so came in 1938 when a small number of us at Harvard met periodically to plumb the contents of *The Marxist Handbook* under the supervision of Granville Hicks. Hicks's appointment in 1939 as one of the eight "Counsellors" in Harvard's extracurricular program to encourage reading in American history outraged the Hearst press and the *Chicago Tribune;* his appearance at a fund-raising event in Cambridge for the Communist *New Masses* ruffled the local press. In an open letter to Boston reporters, Ed Lahey charged that this outcry against Hicks was manufactured for publicity's sake by a few noisy windbags and that the so-called Communist meeting in Cambridge (which had nothing to do with Harvard) was "as interesting as one of your infernal New England clambakes." The hoopla caused no stir in the college. That Hicks happened to be literary editor of a radical magazine was less noteworthy than the fact that he was a Harvard graduate and a former Universalist minister. His vision of what America under Communism might look like, a blend of Brook Farm and Disneyland, was sweet reasonableness itself. In 1938, President Conant predicted that Hicks's "strong leftist views" would invigorate classroom discussions and concluded that to bar him from teaching at Harvard simply because he was a Communist would be "pedagogically" shortsighted as well as bigoted.

With the onset of World War II, Conant reversed himself: never again would he knowingly appoint a Communist to the Harvard faculty. But until Stalin and Hitler signed their non-aggression pact, political discussions at Harvard were, as I remember them, open and unrestrained, and so they were in Granville Hicks's old farmhouse in Grafton, New York. There I met journalists and writers from the "outside world" who appeared in the periodicals I was reading. One of them, John Strachey, the British author of an ingratiating brief for Communism, *The Coming Struggle for Power*, had shown up in Grafton after a brief detention on Ellis Island and was then something of an anomaly, an upper-class Englishman with sophisticated literary tastes and a gift for translating heavy Marxist jargon into vernacular English. But Strachey wasn't thinking about class warfare on one snowy weekend in Hicks's crowded house. Following a day of cross-country skiing, he devoted himself to the pretty and flirtatious wife of one of the guests. A well-lubricated night of carnival ended with an irreverent skit in which she posed naked, a lamb's tail coyly substituting for a fig leaf. Twenty years later, I met Strachey in London. He was then a cabinet member in the Labor government and light-years away from the boisterous randy radical who caroused in Grafton, New York.

Hicks resigned from the Communist Party in 1939 and, for a while, made plans to organize a new non-Communist Left. My friends and I, on the other hand, felt no compulsion to regroup.

We had been more surprised than shocked by the Soviet-German agreement, which seemed to us almost anticlimactic after the collapse of the Spanish Republic half a year earlier. Spain, never Communism, had been our cause. We had cheered every Loyalist advance, grieved over the successes of the insurgents, protested the arms embargo against what we considered the legitimate government of Spain, and cursed what we believed to be the pro-Franco slant of the *New York Times.* Any intimation of Loyalist progress encouraged us. We snatched at crumbs. How immensely heartening it was to learn that the majority of American writers—the good ones—sided with us. *Fascist* was the omnibus epithet for any person or group we considered authoritarian.

If Harvard mostly favored the Spanish Republicans, Greater Boston did not, or so it appeared to me as I watched the police stand by while patriotic Italian-American youths wheeled barrows of rotten vegetables onto the Boston Common and pelted the Reds. The Spanish civil war was long over, the campaign to aid the Spanish refugees was more or less institutionalized, and Generalissimo Francisco Franco himself was entombed before it was possible for me and others to look back at the struggle with a degree of objectivity. Disclosures of Stalin's machinations in Spain corrected historical myopia, yet for me, the ferocious civil war boiled down to the story of a beleaguered people and a Goyaesque sequence of books, films, and paintings: a newspaper photograph of a peasant woman, stoical in her grief, standing with neighbors beside their bombed-out houses; insouciant Barcelona anarchists painting their streetcars bright yellow for no ideological reason apparent to me; a proud and eloquent young miner from the Asturias whom I met in an Amsterdam pub.

When the legitimate Madrid government was still precariously alive, I went to Mechanics Hall (since torn down) in Boston to hear and to watch Granville Hicks take on Father Francis Curran, editor of the *Brooklyn Tablet.* The subject of the debate was the war in Spain. Curran, a smallish vibrant man and ardent ally of Father Charles E. Coughlin, the celebrated "Radio Priest," was admirably designed for demagoguery, and his Coughlinite legions poured in from all over southern New England to hear him orate. They screamed and hugged each other and raised their arms in the Coughlin salute when he materialized on the stage. Curran's thousands blotted out our pitiful claque. Hicks couldn't be heard above the boos and hoots until Curran quieted his disciples and graciously permitted Hicks to make an ineffective pitch. The evening turned into a celebration for Curran, Coughlin, and Franco, a portent of rougher events abroad.

All of this seems marginal now, a historical blink. To me and like-minded friends, it sounded like the trump of doom, and the subsequent events—Munich, the Stalin-Hitler pact, the fall of France—were its inevitable aftermath. By later 1940, our suspicions of the so-called phony war had attenuated to the point where we were prepared, however unenthusiastically, to support a declaration of war against Germany. To us, the Nazis and their allies subsumed all of the wickedness of the world, and any regime in the antifascist camp passed muster.

IV

Nothing in Harvard's American civilization program did much to prepare me for the tidal years ahead, nor did I ever entirely discount the reservations of those who thought it grandiose and chauvinistic. Public spirit flourished in the Depression years, but so did a scoundrelly patriotism. Until enrolled in the new degree, I had kept my studies and my politics in separate compartments. Now the twain converged; the past smelled of the present and the future. For the next few years, I drafted my own chronicle of the American experience and footnoted it with citations from Tocqueville, Vernon L. Parrington, Frederick Jackson Turner, and Charles Beard. I favored and savored the disturbers of the peace, but I also found something bracing in the Puritan theologians and in their conservative legatees.

Entering the program had allowed me to breach departmental boundaries; to take a three-year trip up and down and through undiscovered terrain; to compound history, literature, art, and politics. It offered a passkey to the society I was hoping to burrow into and explore; it legitimated my place and status; it sanctioned my would-be role of explainer of America at home and in foreign parts and encouraged this Americanist to dissolve his psychic hyphen. The long soak in Americana gave me a proprietary feeling about the United States and an urge to excavate what Van Wyck Brooks, whom I was reading at the time, called the "usable past."

In his first books, Brooks made much of the highbrow/lowbrow dichotomy in Puritanical American culture, but by the 1930s, he began to favor (or, as his friend Edmund Wilson put it, to "croon" rapturously over) a tradition he had long disdained. I preferred the acerbic scolding Brooks to Brooks the sweet singer, but I liked his prose style and envied his familiarity with books and authors I had barely heard of, much less read. I was particularly taken with his vision of a landscape crowded with "makers and finders" who confuted tiresome clichés about America. He may have exorcized its lurking terrors, but his vision of a wondrous country—not the machinery-mad, money-mad, soulless land of its debunkers—greatly appealed to me, and I saw less of a gap than was commonly supposed between the Young Turk of the 1910s and 1920s and the antimodernist of the 1950s, sentenced by his juniors to ritual slaughter. Having taken the doctoral examinations for the American civilization program (the first to do so), I was eager to follow the track Brooks had laid down and to look further into the social history of American writers.

PART THREE

I

One spring afternoon in 1939, I opened a telegram from the chairman of Smith College's Department of English. Delivered while
my study group was in session (we were reading *The Marxist
Handbook* at the moment), it contained the offer of a three-year
contract at $2,250 per annum. I recited the message aloud to my
fellows in a ha-ha-what-a-preposterous-notion tone, only to be
put straight by our discussion leader, Granville Hicks. Smith College, he thought I should know, was an exceptional place. He had
taught there, and Newton Arvin, whom he knew I greatly
admired, still did. Reassured, but uneasy at the prospect of teaching at a women's college and not expecting to stay at Smith longer
than two or three years at most, I wired my acceptance. I
remained at Smith, albeit with frequent and lengthy leaves of
absence, for the next thirty years, turning down invitations to
move elsewhere.

The ghost of Warren G. Harding's successor, Calvin
Coolidge, was still walking the streets of Northampton,
Massachusetts, when I got there in the fall of 1939. Six years after
his death, his aura had clouded, and he was already undergoing
the shriveling process that awaits all but the superpresidents. Yet
as he diminished, he still retained a qualified distinction as a
canny, laconic, and commonsensical Yankee—a relic of a simpler
America. One photograph of Vice President Coolidge and Presi-

dent Harding shows them seated in adjoining chairs: Harding, the aging actor, looks at ease with the world; Coolidge, the foxy veep, his face fresh and unlined, looks like the head teller of a small-town bank, not yet resembling the alleged hypochondriac who Ike Hoover described in his reminiscences as working less and sleeping more than any of the presidents Hoover had known. In another photograph, this one in the Coolidge Room of Northampton's wonderful Forbes Library, Coolidge is seated in a rowboat. Coatless but wearing a shirt and tie and a straw hat, he holds up a pole to which a fish seems to be fixed.

Many stories bruited in Northampton contributed to Coolidge's quirky legend. You could trace the steps he took from his more-than-comfortable house on Washington Avenue, not far from where I later lived, to his office. My neighbor Mr. Niquette, a druggist who lived across the street, set them out for me. Every morning, said Mr. Niquette, Coolidge would stop for him, and the two of them would stroll down Washington Avenue to Elm Street, thence southward past the college, past the Catholic church, deflecting left as Elm Street melted into Main. Mr. Niquette told me that Coolidge didn't talk much, that he really was "Silent Cal." Their ritual walk ended with an eye-opener at the Draper Hotel, two shots for a half-dollar. Coolidge would drink one of his in the morning and return for the dividend in the later afternoon, before silently heading home with Mr. Niquette in tow.

No one I knew in Northampton spoke of Coolidge with affection. One elderly gossip fed me anecdotes about his parsimony and meanness: how he had once stuffed his erring cat into a gunnysack and hung it from a beam in his garage; how he was responsible for the death of his son, John. According to the gossip's preposterous tale, Coolidge forced his son to keep reversing his left and right shoes so that they would wear more evenly; hence John developed the blister that killed him. These and other apocryphal stories, most of them uncomplimentary, support the popular image of the caustic taciturn sage.

Some of the blinkered impressions of Coolidge, the parochial and complacent man "weaned on a pickle," linger in the outrageous parodies of H. L. Mencken, Sinclair Lewis, and Nathanael West. While still in office, he had already become a national character, a type of "cute Yankee" and source of comic anecdotes. His wife fared better. Grace Coolidge pleased the public and remained popular. I first associated her with the Girl Scout cookie campaigns she sponsored, and I came to like her as the quiet genial woman who would drive with a crony to Boston to watch the Red Sox play and who was pleasant to my sons. The memory of her mitigates the sour reputation of Northampton's former mayor, the former governor of Massachusetts, and the thirtieth president of the United States. ❦

Northampton's location and manageable size seemed likely to suit me and my wife, Janet, very well. It was close to places we wanted to be close to by train and car, and there were other reasons as well, as it turned out, for our growing attachment to the college and the town. Having lived since 1924 in what I came to think of as a sequence of temporary campsites, I would for the first time become a recognizable townsman, a familiar to storekeepers, service people, businessmen, politicians, and policemen. I would at last be freely rooted in a community that accepted me as a college teacher, an honorable alien.

To inspect and be inspected and to get our first look at Smith College, my wife and I drove to Northampton in her father's shiny red Lincoln. We parked it some distance from the college, embarrassed by its spread of chrome, and walked to the president's modest office. William Allan Neilson (1869–1946), one of the last of a line of notable college presidents, was about to retire. A wise and winning Scotsman and a respected Shakespearean scholar, he had come to Smith via Harvard in 1917 and had been its resourceful and parsimonious manager for years, with a knack for recruiting his international faculty on the cheap. Smith teachers spoke English in a variety of foreign accents, and a lot of French, Italian, and German (the last the native tongue of Mrs. Neilson) could be heard on Main Street. President Neilson was well liked on the whole, and his quips were part of college lore, but a number of Northamptonians didn't quite know what to make of him. He added luster to the city, but he had been much criticized in some quarters for allowing Smith students to demonstrate against the executions of Sacco and Vanzetti in 1927. Crazy Elizabeth Dilling included him, along with Eleanor Roosevelt, in her notorious *The Red Network* (1935). For me, the liberal aura he cast made Smith, in contrast to buttoned-up Amherst College nearby, seem almost raffishly international.

Neilson interviewed me in the old-fashioned president's office he occupied with his "staff," an omniscient secretary grown old in her job. He asked me what I thought of Newton Arvin's new book on Whitman, which he considered (rightly, I now believe) to be inferior or at least more tendentious than Arvin's earlier study of Hawthorne. I argued so heatedly to the contrary that I thought I queered myself, but for him it was probably an ordinary exchange. He must have been one of the last of the college presidents to read the publications of his faculty.

On May 30, 1940, before the Japanese attack on Pearl Harbor, before the Battle of Britain, before the *Wehrmacht* smashed through France and the Low Countries, I wrote what I called "A Note to Posterity" in my journal.

What it's like to be alive in the spring of 1940. I speak of a twenty-eight-year-old man who is waiting for something to happen, getting ready for it. His feelings of fear, apprehension, resignation mixed with joy, excitement, and anticipation. He's going toward "something" expectantly, eyes open wide. The great slide is beginning, the momentum speeding up, brakes off. The radio is always on. One grows used to the announcement of catastrophes, not merely little inconsequential ones, but big ones too. Whir of arms production. Bombs, bullets, tanks, planes pour off assembly lines. Warnings of invasions from hysterical South America, from Japan, of troops by the millions parachuting down from the swollen sky. We must build up the fleet, produce more and faster planes. Make twelve hundred a day. Ford says he can. Knudson doesn't doubt it. "Fifth columnist," a term which may seem quaint in five hundred years or less. Now it connotes treachery and violence; soon it will become a smear word applied to anyone who holds unpopular opinions.

Americans in 1940 go to ball games, dances, parties, movies, art galleries as I do. We don't lacerate ourselves because thousands of people abroad are being blown to bits. We don't hang a piece of gigantic crepe over the country. No policy, no direction for the moment, a disregard for coming terror. Anyone will be lucky who thirty years from now can drink a glass of orange juice and smoke a cigarette—I mean anyone my age.

Several months after that entry, I reported without comment, "Japan bombed Pearl Harbor," and after I failed an eye test for a navy commission, I readied myself for the inevitable draft. "Teaching haphazardly, waiting for the army to take me," reads a journal entry for December 2, 1942, which continues, "I want to join and be overwhelmed with a little experience." I was convinced that my age (over thirty) and marital and paternal status (wife and one child) would only briefly postpone the summons to war. Twice I notified Smith College that I had been reclassified and would soon be in the army. The call never came.

II

Northampton signified for me two independent and, on occasion, hostile entities: the college and the town. Until the all-male colleges and universities admitted women against the dwindling resistance of a good many diehards, Smith and its sister institutions—Bryn Mawr, Mount Holyoke, Vassar, Barnard, Wellesley, and Radcliffe—were the complements of the Ivy League's men's colleges. Each had its gossip-based distinctions: Vassar, debutantish-artistic-literary; Bryn Mawr and Radcliffe, serious-scholarly; Mount Holyoke, clergymanish-mousy; Wellesley, socially safe and respectable; Barnard, dun-colored and nondescript; Smith, politically and sexually liberal and the least regional of the "Seven Sisters." (Bennington College, which my wife attended in its first two years and where I moonlighted in 1951 and 1952, was a different kettle of fish. It had a special appeal for the self-absorbed and casually reared children of the well-heeled. At times it suggested an affluent and permissive asylum in which the teachers doubled as priests, psychiatrists, counselors, and companions. A number of them lived on college grounds so that student-faculty commingling, both academic and informal, was frequent and fluid. At one party, the poet Theodore Roethke, ordinarily a peaceable fellow with whom I used to play horseshoes in Ann Arbor, got quite drunk and kept throwing punches at me as I stood in the middle of a stairway trying to fend him off from a student he was pursuing.)

Comparable excitements were rarer at Smith College. Spreading over a low elevation above the town center a few miles west of the usually well-behaved Connecticut River and safe from its occasional flooding, Smith had less of the picture-postcard "Ivy" look of so many New England colleges It was also unpretentious and latitudinarian and "natural." The majority of Smith students, like those in other private colleges for women, came from comfortable and conservative backgrounds and tended to grow piously tolerant and open-minded between their freshman and senior years. A scattering of radicals leavened the student lump, but their protests were more likely to be social than political. A few unserious and clubby societies might provoke mild dissent from the excluded on occasion, but with little rancor, for the college was too large and diverse and tolerant to sustain bitter divisions. Smith students, quartered in Victorian cottage-houses on and off the campus and in gracious rectangular residence halls, behaved like members of an extended family. The few African-American women were well received for the most part and sometimes aggressively coerced into taking high office. Students as different as Victoria Schrager, Betty Friedan, Jane White, Gloria Steinem, Aileen Ward, and Sylvia Plath graduated from Smith during my tenure, not one of them typical, yet each in her way a product of the college.

If collectively unastonishing, Smith women were hardheaded, resourceful, practical, and disciplined, or so it seemed to me. They were less romantic and sentimental than their men friends, who more often than not were impervious to irony and less adroit in combining their academic and social business. Smith "girls" turned into women faster than the "boys" they dated turned into men, and the best of them positively glittered as they performed their academic assignments. Yet these same confident students accepted what had not yet been labeled "male hegemony" without noticeable protest; they showed little interest in the history of their sex and adapted themselves to the assumptions and values of their clunky consorts. It was hard to square their aptitudes and intelligence with their passion for engagement rings and matrimony. Once, in a moment of misogynistic exasperation, Newton Arvin peevishly called them "tarts," but more than a few, he conceded, were "as good as the country affords." One can only speculate on the social costs of the "feminine mystique" that conditioned so many gifted women to their comfortable purdahs.

In 1939, when I arrived, women made up a slight majority of the Smith faculty. The oldest of the emeritae were such relics as Elizabeth Hanscomb, who had taught one of the first American literature courses in the country some time in the 1890s. Miss Hanscomb told me that as a little girl in Maine, she dived between the legs of Harriet Beecher Stowe while the old lady patted the water with diamonded fingers. Another pioneer—and a tough one—was Miss Cobb, a former math teacher, who died in her eighties, leaving one hundred thousand dollars to relatives and to the local Congregational church and nothing to Smith, although the college had long endured her pestiferous ways in the expectation of getting a legacy. She would sit in the periodical room of the William Allen Nielson Library, her false teeth clacking audibly as she read. She wet the chairs of the Browsing Room so that they had to be recovered, chiseled stamps, and bummed nickels for telephone calls. I can see her now, patient, furtive, her brown face unlined, her gray hair pulled back. She walked with a cane yet briskly enough, padding around the library in sneakers—accompanied always by the dreadful clacking of teeth.

These women and their young successors tended to be hard on themselves, not overly protective of their sisters, undeferential to their male colleagues, and models for their students. The triple names of these teachers and scholars seemed as set in bronze as those of their male peers. They challenged the spinster stereotype, resolutely kept abreast of the new, and although decorous themselves, were unflummoxed by the indecorous. "I have lived, Dan—oh, I've lived," Esther Cloudman Dunn once said to me as she angled successfully to obtain what was still called the "chairmanship" of the college's Department of English. She was no Wife of Bath, but I believed her.

A trio of other women I came to know pretty well are emblematic of that time and place. What turned into a long and affectionate friendship began shortly after I found myself the only male teaching a section in Mary Ellen Chase's introductory course in English composition. At the end of our first staff meeting, she invited the "girls" to join her for a Coke. (I associate the day with a tortuous hunt for the room marked "GENTLEMEN," cunningly concealed under a stairway in the basement of the William Allen Neilson Library.) Miss Chase lived in a white, box-shaped New England cottage on Paradise Road with Eleanor Duckett, her longtime friend, a graduate of Cambridge University and a professor of classics. Miss Chase wasn't Duckett's kind of scholar. She wrote popular fiction and nonfiction, which she invariably pooh-poohed, for a substantial company of fans and for substantial sums of money. "Don't you dare read it!" she would say about some piece soon to appear in *Reader's Digest*.

I could never bring myself to call Miss Chase "Mary," as some of my younger colleagues did, but somehow she made me feel cherished and important, a key member of her faction. I think she felt that I brought some credit to the college that over the years had become an extension of herself. She told me stories about her Maine childhood; her young womanhood in Madison, Wisconsin; and her dislike for Frank Lloyd Wright. I gathered that Wright had once made a pass at her, which she indignantly rejected. Perhaps he was attracted by the virginal prettiness she still retained when I knew her. Letters in my "M. E. Chase" file describe her sojourn at Cambridge University to study Hebrew in preparation for her widely read book on the Bible as literature, her trips to France and Spain, and a memorable account of a weekend with the Aga Khan in the Maritime Alps. I had asked her to write to me about the man who had himself periodically weighed on a scale balanced with sacks of diamonds (or so it was said), and she did. That letter and others she wrote to me portray Miss Chase in all of her innocence, vanity, enthusiasm, goodness, and generosity. Her pomposities were angelic. At home in the houses of rich admirers, the Rockefellers and Morrows among them, Miss Chase was pleased to discover sterling qualities in her hosts that diverted attention from their acquisitive forebears.

Off and on, Miss Chase summoned me to her house for ritual breakfasts. After she had bustled Miss Duckett, whom she lovingly exploited, off to the library, we would hash over departmental matters and national politics. Usually we were in accord, her rock-ribbed Republican origins notwithstanding; she was conscientiously "liberal" and opposed to what she thought I opposed and scorned. Both of us supported Adlai Stevenson for president, but Miss Chase audibly wondered what he could possibly see in Dorothy Fosdick, then a member of Smith's Department of Government and the daughter of the prominent New York clergyman and radio preacher Harry Emerson Fosdick of Rockefeller's Riverside Church. Miss Chase hinted that she had information about a shadowy affair, but she never divulged any of it to me. She was less reserved about her hostility to the Luce magazines and to the congressional investigators rooting up the radical pasts of a few Smith College professors. Newton Arvin awed her, or at least his reputation did. Very likely she had heard more about his not-so-secret pastimes than she cared to know, yet she respected my respect for him.

Miss Chase kept her unassailable position at Smith without offending her queenly rivals or the junior people on the faculty whose tastes and interests were more outré than her own. One such person was Mina Curtiss, who had been a student at Smith in the closing years of World War I. She joined the faculty in the early 1920s, after the death of her husband, to whom she continued sending messages for a time via her pieces in the *Atlantic Monthly*. Student gossip had it that she kept a black panther in her rooms, a rumor she did nothing to discourage, for she wasn't your ordinary lady professor. Through her brother, Lincoln Kirstein, onetime editor of the avant-garde *Hound and Horn*, she came into contact with people worldlier than her teachers and peers. Their father owned Filene's, a Boston department store, and she could easily afford to live stylishly, dress expensively, and travel where and when she pleased. By the time I met her, she was a kind of indecorous bluestocking, a friend and summer neighbor of Archibald MacLeish in nearby Ashville.

Mina introduced me to Wystan Auden, her guest at the time and shortly to be a visiting professor at Smith (he advised me to read Søren Kierkegaard) and to the amusing stage designer Aline Bernstein, onetime inamorata of Thomas Wolfe and the Esther Jack in his novel *You Can't Go Home Again*. (Forty-five years later, Lillian Hellman, then half alive, plagued to death with emphysema but still very far from pitiful, told me what Bernstein had told her about Wolfe's kinky antics. "Come out, you dirty Jew, and fuck," he would call out as he paced the corridor outside of her hotel. Hellman, who had taken a course from Wolfe and remembered him as physically dangerous, ordered her friend to stop telling her these stories, with the argument that in repeating them, Bernstein was more shameful than Wolfe.) It was no secret at Smith that Mina bowed in and out of Wolfe's roman à clef as Lily Mandell, the "heiress of Midas wealth," a "dark statuesque" beauty with "heavy-lidded eyes," whose "tall and voluptuous figure" seemed literally to have been "poured" into her magnificent gown.

The Mina who befriended me in the early 1940s didn't look much like Wolfe's sultry houri, but she retained something of her spoiled, youthful, generous, and vulnerable self. She had fulfilled, as she wrote thirty years later, "one of those adolescent fantasies in which one imagines oneself in the center of some romantic yet realistically perceived scene—the 'Belle of the Ball' in short." She was living that role when I first met her. Like many forceful and ambitious people, Mina hadn't a smidgen of self-irony. She exploited her modest gifts, moved in high-toned circles, alluded to her private adventures, and cultivated the well-connected. In time, she became a pastiche of the grand people and celebrities and artists she had met—a kind of Sargasso Sea.

None of my other women colleagues, no matter how eminent, exuded a comparable glamour, but not even Mina could match the glitter of Katherine Anne Porter, who flashed through the college like a comet. Newton Arvin had invited her, but in his absence, I was obliged to entertain her. She touched off a mild commotion not only because she tried unsuccessfully to cram her novella *Pale Horse, Pale Rider* into an afternoon's reading but also because of the spell she cast on the male members of the Department of English after her performance. They clustered around her like honeybees, leaving the local lionesses to pace up and down my long living room unattended and discomfited.

Mina Curtis had just quit the Northampton scene when Elizabeth Drew, a slim, handsome Englishwoman with a manner just a touch chilly and a comic sensibility like Jane Austen's, began her long stint at Smith in the fall of 1943. We had met two years earlier, at Middlebury College's summer Bread Loaf School of English in Vermont, where she had been the star lecturer. Separated from her husband, a Cambridge don, she had brought her young son to the States to escape the Blitz and was teaching at a girls' school in Farmington, Connecticut, when a sun-blinded truck driver ran over him. "No, there isn't anything to say," she replied to my letter of condolence, adding: "One had to remind one's self one is one of millions in the same situation—that there are also millions of women who would give anything for the 14 years I had. It makes no difference to the heartbreak but keeps me from self-pity." At Smith, where she elegantly aged, she took comfort in the community of affectionate students and confessed to some pleasure in contrasting her own physical state with that of many people slightly younger than herself but more infirm: "It struck me how it is really gracelessness of movement that is the chief sign of age. After about 60, even if not on crutches, most women begin to be lumbering; they waddle or shuffle, or drag or heave themselves about, which is very unattractive. Men don't seem to suffer from it so much! And I am glad to say that though my back plagues me incessantly, I'm still light and limber."

Elizabeth Drew never strayed from the Anglo-American social and literary circles and was my friend and critic for more than twenty years. I associate her with particular moments, especially with the Vermont summer of 1941, when a group of us (it included the poet John Crowe Ransom and a gently derisive graduate assistant, Richard Ellmann) would troop up to Robert Frost's house nearby and listen to his ruminations. Slumped back in an easy chair, his old Vermont collie at his feet, Frost would ramble on, his voice low and drowsy. There was nothing of the show-off in these soliloquies as there was so often in his public performances, whether on the lecture platform or the softball field. I don't remember asking what Elizabeth really thought of his poetry, but she must have been irritated by his snide digs at T. S. Eliot, whom she admired above all modern poets. Her tastes and connections remained English. I think the foreign-born faculty at Smith were expected to retain their respective accents and national mannerisms. After forty years in Northampton, some of my French colleagues still spoke English through a thick impasto of their mother tongue, while I, a foreigner of a different sort, dug deeper into the western Massachusetts terrain.

III

What amounted to a long probation as a town citizen started after the Japanese attack on Pearl Harbor, when I hired myself out to Polish farmers on the eastern side of the Connecticut River. Patriotism spurred me, but so did the possibility that hard physical work and no reading would improve my eyesight enough to pass the eye test for a navy commission. Early in the century, Polish families had emigrated to the Connecticut Valley from the Pennsylvania coal districts and bought land from the dwindling number of Yankees in the Hatfield-Hadley-Amherst area. Now, short on manpower because of the war, they gladly hired untrained hands like me in the summer months at twenty-five cents an hour, to cut, bunch, and pack asparagus ("grass" in the local vernacular); to sucker and chop tobacco plants before hanging them in suffocating barns; and to harvest potatoes—the hardest and dirtiest operation of the lot.

Most of my coworkers were high school kids. It took a lot of getting used to before they accepted the superannuated greenhorn (me) and stopped swiping his lunch. (I did nothing to get back at them then, but at the end of the summer—and to everyone's amusement—I grabbed the ringleader and sat him on top of a drinking fountain.) Their elders addressed them in Galician Polish—rather like Ukrainian, I was told—and they replied in an ugly bastard English, for they had junked the ancestral tongue without having properly learned a new one. Only after a year's stay in Poland in 1962–63 did I get an inkling of Polish language and literature—though not for want of opportunity. The wife of a refugee scholar, Manfred Kridl, had urged me to study Polish with her instead of studying Russian. My colleague Jane Zielonko, the smart and vivacious daughter of a Polish priest, also volunteered to give me lessons. It was she who brought her friend Czesław Miłosz to our house late one night shortly before he quit the Polish embassy and broke his party chains. In the fall of 1950, Jane and I campaigned for Congressman (and later Massachusetts governor) Foster Furcolo—I at the wheel of a hired sound truck that played a jingle I'd written to the tune of a Pepsi-Cola musical ad, she broadcasting in Polish over the loudspeaker system to astonished farmers working in the tobacco fields.

Politics, like farming, was serious business in Northampton and its environs and preoccupied a lot of people, including me. The old-stock local gentry occupying the best houses usually voted Republican, but so did small contingents of people with Polish and French-Canadian names. The Irish pretty well decided what was what in Democratic Party politics. The small community of Jews wasn't solidly of either party but shaded toward the Democrats. The same was true of my fellow academics, though most of them didn't bother much with local and state politics or take time to weigh the qualifications of the candidates. They came to my wife and me for political dope, and because we inadvertently "controlled" a large bundle of votes in Northampton's silk-stocking district, the Democratic pols deemed us worthy of recognition. During election times, the state and national candidates paid visits to our kitchen for tips on useful contacts. Foster Furcolo came with his campaign manager Larry O'Brien (soon to be JFK's trusted aide), and we were visited by Adlai Stevenson, who was adored by the students of the Ivy League. On election day, I checked lists of registered Democrats, telephoned the apathetic, hauled the faithful to and from the polls, and took on other kinds of bread-and-butter party work. Among Northampton's notable Democrats was another "foreigner," the widow of the once eminent historian John Spencer Bassett. Her husband had been fired from Trinity College (soon to become Duke University) for his liberal views on the "Negro question" and was promptly invited to teach at Smith. Mrs. Bassett, a regal Virginia lady in her late seventies, wore her white hair like a turban and pronounced the word *card* as if it were spelled "kyard." She lived in a Victorian Gothic house, behind which a well-tended lawn rolled down to the river. An old retainer cultivated her small vineyard and bottled her quite agreeable wine. Come election day, she commandeered the polling booth in her ward and bossed her dutiful helpers. She was the grandest Democrat in the city.

There were moments when my party coworkers—particularly the acolytes of Cardinal Spellman, Joseph McCarthy, and Father Curran—nauseated the Northampton Democrats of my wing. We were fed up with interparty squabbles over recognition and with family feuds transported from Ireland years before and still festering. Hence I was strongly tempted to desert my greedy, benighted, and self-serving associates and to consider Republican alternatives—at least for local and state offices. I'd grown to like my neighbor Judge Rufus Cook, a crusty anti–New Dealer who was nonetheless so stunned by FDR's unexpected death that he took to his bed for a day. I liked Grace Coolidge, the president's serene and unaffected widow, who lived down the street. I valued the friendship of the public-spirited bank president, who was also an ingrained conservative. But after casing the political meetings of the Northampton Republicans and watching them collectively at play, I felt irrevocably bound to the blowsy Democrats.

Political partnership subsided in the city as the war against Hitler and Hirohito made all other issues pale. The remote, inscrutable, and outlandish Japanese made ideal enemies. Cartoonists transformed them into short, bowlegged, slant-eyed, bucktoothed monkeys, at once savage and ridiculous. Common knowledge had it that everything they made quickly fell to pieces. Mr. Niquette, my druggist neighbor, assured me that one American marine more than matched fifteen "Japs." The war in the Pacific soon expunged such folklore, but stories of Japanese cruelty, a good many of them authenticated, strengthened the popular belief that the Japanese were subhuman. Thus it happened that when Smith recruited a Japanese-born "alien"—Dr. Shuichi

Kusaka—to teach in its depleted physics department, the college was angrily assailed by a crowd of indignant locals. Kusaka himself, a noble fellow who had repudiated the Japanese militarists and who was commended by the American government and by national educational agencies, was abused on Northampton streets. An anonymous phone caller berated me for playing tennis with this treacherous "Nip."

In Northampton, any public affronter of popular prejudice courted censure. I found this out again in 1951, after criticizing Joe McCarthy before a joint meeting of the Rotary and Kiwanis clubs. One man whispered as he passed me, eyes straight ahead, that he was glad I had spoken out, but no one in that stony-faced audience applauded. I was taken aback but shouldn't have been. The club members were part of a national contingent that had given a hero's welcome to General Douglas MacArthur, just fired by President Truman for pushing his private war against China; they had driven their cars up and down Northampton's streets, headlights ablaze, horns honking.

After tumbling into the presidency on April 12, 1945, the day FDR died, Harry S. Truman authorized the Hiroshima and Nagasaki bombs, lent his name to a doctrine, backed the fateful plan of his secretary of state George C. Marshall, supervised the Korean War (or UN police action), and sacked MacArthur for insubordination. These events, some of which I deplored, some of which I cheered, flicker in my journal, as does Truman himself as he steps out from behind Roosevelt's shadow, looking too small and humble to handle the job ahead, the prototypical "little man" who succeeds a titan. His tight double-breasted business suits breathe Independence, Missouri. In one photograph, he stands between the meaty, uniformed Stalin and Churchill, who might be his prison guards. The Englishman holds an unlit cigar; the dictator is about to light up. Neither shows the slightest interest in the mousy American.

Yet my first impressions of Truman had been cautiously positive. He had ably chaired a committee to investigate defense contracts. His debt to the unsavory Kansas City Pendergast machine meant less to me than what I took to be his populist sensibility and his deep-dyed distrust of corporate America's leadership. I still tended to judge politicians by their friends and enemies, and the news I monitored and digested reflected my left-liberal biases and provided the lowdown to counteract the Republican right wing.

In 1946, I was teaching a course on American political thought and doing research on a book that, thanks to a Guggenheim Foundation grant, would be published as *Men of Good Hope: A Story of American Progressives* (1951). I had planned to end it with Henry Wallace (then, in my opinion, the Progressive Era's last representative) until I learned that some of the ringing speeches ascribed to him had been ghosted. As the 1948 presidential campaign got under way, I found myself slowly moving from the Wallace camp to the Truman camp, put off in part by the faux-naïf "American" line the Communists were orchestrating for the new Progressive Party and by Dwight Macdonald's withering appraisals of Wallace and his legions, published in his magazine Politics. By September 1948, I had joined the Americans for Democratic Action, an organization of the non-Communist Left, and decided to vote for Norman Thomas, the Socialist Party's perennial candidate. On election day, for pragmatic (rather than principled) reasons, I put my mark by Truman's name on the ballot and told no one. The next evening, I met Norman Thomas at the apartment of a mutual friend in East-hampton, Massachusetts. He was amused that Dewey had lost despite the predictions of the pollsters, and Thomas had nothing harsh to say about the victor.

I continued to serve as a foot soldier in the Truman ranks, but my enthusiasm waned after the congressional primitives and their abettors pushed through a loyalty program that seemed to people like me more threatening to American democracy than did the moth-eaten remnants of the American Communist Party. I stuck to the Truman who desegregated the armed services and fired the Olympian MacArthur. I sympathized with the cocky, cheerful paterfamilias who threatened to beat up a

Washington music critic for dumping on the singing debut of his daughter, Margaret. Like Fiorello LaGuardia, Truman might have been the hero of an American musical comedy. His GOP detractors and Thomas Dewey, his overconfident opponent, mis-assessed or failed to acknowledge his republican virtues, his uncommon commonality. It would have pleased me to meet him on one of his much-reported walks on the streets of New York, to greet him as "Mr. President," to ask him if I might join the little gang that accompanied him, to raise a point or two in American history and perhaps even venture a disagreement. (It was well known, he told Arthur M. Schlesinger Jr., that Mark Twain wrote Grant's memoirs.) If he didn't have a rich and copious mind or radiate nobility, he encouraged a trust in Herman Melville's "great democratic God," who had picked Harry Truman from the pebbles and hurled him into the White House.

General Dwight D. Eisenhower's elevation in 1952 was less fortuitous. He was already a "great man." The shortening of his middle name, *David,* to an initial gave his name a hard and soldier-like edge; the sobriquet "Ike" suited the tough fatherly face that Norman Rockwell universalized on the cover of the *Saturday Evening Post.* The supreme commander of the Allied armies on the Western Front had behaved less like a generalissimo than a placatory majordomo as flamboyant generals and salty admirals moved center stage. Eisenhower wasn't given to grandiloquence in the manner of his swashbuckling peers, and he eschewed plumage. Not until his postwar extramilitary stirrings did I and my counterparts realize with a certain uneasiness that he had political ambitions. We fixed our hopes on his Democratic Party opponent, the governor of Illinois, in the coming presidential election. Adlai E. Stevenson had charmed my wife and me when he stopped at our house during his first presidential campaign (as members of the Democratic City Committee, we were deemed worthy of this recognition), but how naive of us to think that he had a chance to defeat the general. It should have been obvious that his popularity with eggheads would turn off the men in the street. He was too intellectually playful and too ironic and witty and articulate to compete on even terms with a war hero who spoke in the language and accents of "real" America and who looked like one of the players (circa 1910–20) in my old baseball card collection. Ike's promise to go to Korea, the charges (overblown and partisan) of corruption in the Truman government, the rising fear of Communism, and sheer public inertia floated him into office. I mourned Stevenson's predictable annihilation.

In time, I deglamorized Stevenson without ceasing to admire him. It took longer to take Ike's proper measure and to see him as a larger figure in American history than people like me once pegged him. Often, he appeared too cautious and too politic, too ready to concede Senator McCarthy growing room, and too fastidious (as he famously put it) to "tussle with skunks." Maybe my intense dislike of the Republican Party and a perception that Eisenhower's famous "engaging grin" hid something not so nice made us distrust his judgments on many delicate and difficult issues. I could never in good conscience have worn an "I Like Ike" button, for then I considered him a GOP true believer and a political incompetent. Interviews with him quoted in the *New York Times* were miracles of incoherence, and we would read them aloud to savor their ineptitudes. His supporters claimed that he coined these graceless sentences to obfuscate hostile reporters and that his thoughts came too fast for him to articulate them. All the same, he had no trouble saying what he wanted to say and saying it clearly. For me, President Eisenhower was always General Eisenhower in mufti and was never more remote than when smiling down on dutiful crowds and mechanically hoisting his arms. Only after he had given his farewell address and begun to state openly what he had guardedly intimated—namely, the threat of a military-industrial complex—did I begin to have a degree of insight into his knotty character. I also suspected, with no evidence to back me, that he preferred his young successor to his own creepy veep. ☝

By the war's end, I had crossed the line dividing town and college by pitching for the Purseglove Pups, a softball team organized by the owner of a local bicycle shop, and by joining the

Northampton Auxiliary Police. I wore a helmet and carried a billy club while keeping the streets safe during blackouts and hurricanes. Sergeant O'Donnell, a retired state police officer, conducted a series of training sessions and showed us how to twist the arm of a reluctant prisoner when carting him off to jail, how to club him on the neck and shoulder where it wouldn't show, and how to calm him down by stamping on his toes. "Everyone has a corn," the sergeant assured us, but we had no chance to apply his instructions or do much more than turn out at prescribed times. After the auxilliary police disbanded in 1946, my friends in the Northampton Police Department advised me to quit the college and join the force.

IV

In 1960, a story flared up in the tabloid press across the country that entangled Smith College and the Massachusetts State Police, shook up American academia, and did in my colleague, mentor, and friend Newton Arvin. He had been the main inducement for my coming to Smith twenty years before; now he and two other members of the college faculty were being charged with the possession of pornographic material. I walked with Newton to the Northampton Court House on a September morning. The trial was held in a large chamber. A robed judge was on a dais, and around him were faceless clerks and stenographers and a sprinkling of gawkers. If there were photographers and reporters at these low-keyed proceedings, I don't remember them. What I do remember is the tense and white-faced defendant sitting next to me, my feeling of have been plunked down in an alien space, the piles of "obscene" magazines stacked on a table below the judge's bench, a droning voice stating the charges, and my sense that none of the defenders or prosecutors relished the assignment.

The man on trial was no stranger to the town, no shoddy bum. He was a Smith College professor, a respectable figure well known to local merchants and shopkeepers, doctors, and bank officials. A walker of Northampton streets, he seldom went bareheaded and was always well groomed—his suits pressed, his ties discreet, his shoes shined. He was immensely polite, a hat tipper. He wore rubbers when it rained and looked and behaved at times like the cartoon character the Timid Soul; but he took tremendous risks when out cruising or checking the men's room in the Springfield bus station a short distance away. Newton Arvin was a timorous man but a bold thinker, whose contradictions I never managed to sort out, much less comprehend. I simply regarded him as a rare creature (fearful, rash, selfish, generous, petty, tender, secretive), an intrepid intellectual explorer (this character detectible, I thought, in his strong slashing calligraphy) disguised as Caspar Milquetoast. Born Frederic Newton Arvin in Valparaiso, Indiana, he had dropped his first name by the time he graduated from Harvard College, but he clung to his Midwestern roots. He was serious but unsolemn, his humor droll rather than uproarious. He had an eye and ear for the ludicrous. His prime targets were likely to be specimens from the fauna of the academy, "our contemporary Scholastics and Dryasdusts," with "no more notion of what literature is all about than a mole has of astronomy." They made him, he said, "eager to be 'impressionistic,' 'intuitional,' 'appreciative,' 'unsystematic,' and all the other sins of their tight little Eliotine Decalogue." He kept his literary antipathies under wraps, however, and paid homage to writers and critics he genuinely admired and deferred to. One of them was his old friend and patron Van Wyck Brooks, whose antimodernism he deplored, but who remained for him the "only man we have who can tell off the pedants."

By the later 1940s, Arvin had soured (I quote from his letters) on "the hard-boiled or the 'objective' or the tough-minded school of my generation" (James T. Farrell once told me that Newton wrote well but "had corsets around his tastes and curiosities"). Arvin had come to feel "infinitely more at home" with younger writers, notably the lyrical Gothicist Carson McCullers, whom he loved and worried over, and the "wonderfully gifted youth named Truman Capote," a tropical bird who for a short time flew in and out of Northampton and affected Arvin in some of the same ways McCullers did. Although he rarely spoke of his liaisons, casual or intimate, Arvin took pains to remind me that the word *gay* now meant something more than "cheerful" and "merry." I think he believed that, at bottom, every man would recognize his latent homosexuality if he dug deep enough into his nature, and I suspect he was disappointed by my obtuseness about such things. It was easier for him to discuss his extracurricular adventures with our colleague Alfred Young Fisher, a poet-scholar closer to him in age and an unflappable listener to stories of his sexual adventures. To many in and outside the college, Fisher was as much a "character" as Newton himself, distinguished by his baroque mannerisms and old-fashioned locutions and well known for his custom (a legacy of his student days in France) of reading and writing in the local bistros. For thirty years, between his three marriages, he charmed a number of Smith women into his bed, but he was always the teacher concerned with their education, no matter how unconventional his pedagogy. He gave considerable time and thought to cookery (his first wife was the writer-gastronome M. F. K. Fisher), and he could turn an egg or potato into a poem. While at Smith, he annotated the texts of *Ulysses* and *Finnegans Wake* with the zeal of a medieval grammarian. He was invariably generous and loyal to me and a small group of friends and regarded Newton Arvin as both a dark figure cocooned in selfishness and a precious vessel to be treasured and watched over. We might have laughed at Newton's hypochondria, yet we trusted him (and rightly so), as a family member who loved and rewarded us in his own self-regarding way.

I hadn't known, as I sat with Newton in the Northampton courtroom and glowered at the meaty-faced Sergeant John T. Regan, chief of the pornography unit of the Massachusetts State Police, that the raid on his flat had been a spin-off of the "Stamp Out Smut" campaign launched by President Eisenhower's postmaster general, Arthur E. Summerville. A state law passed in 1959 had changed an obscenity offense from a misdemeanor to a felony and had given the state police the power to set up a bureau designed to ferret out and prosecute "pornographers," thus enabling Sergeant Regan and his men to break into Arvin's apartment on Prospect Street and ransack his files in search of obscene material.

A long and interesting history lay behind the efforts of the Commonwealth of Massachusetts to protect its citizens from moral pollution. The state commissioner of safety J. Henry Gorguen and Sergeant Regan were only the latest of Massachusetts's public guardians to protect the moral weal of the public. They pictured themselves as kindly and welcomed redeemers. As Regan confided to reporters, here were all these educated people—college professors and the like—who knew they were doing wrong and were often relieved when they got caught, because their detection ended the haunting fear of blackmail. Most of the delinquents, said Regan, were humbled and ashamed; it was all the more important, then, that the investigators carry on their therapeutic work disinterestedly yet with pity. The sergeant certainly had a model (if ungrateful) lawbreaker in Newton Arvin, whom he first scared to death and then got to implicate his gay friends. I knew nothing at the time about Newton's singing to the police, but I would have been too familiar with his anxieties and terrors to condemn his behavior. Charged with lewdness and the possession of obscene material, he pled guilty and was fined twelve hundred dollars and given a one-year suspended sentence.

Not to be minimized in this sorry tale is the conspiratorial atmosphere of the time and the McCarthyist fog that had settled thickly over the Republic. In the mind of the Wisconsin senator (or, at any rate, in McCarthy's public utterances), Communism and homosexuality were kindred diseases. Newton had had some cause to worry that an exhumation of his early radical associations might turn up evidence that he was gay. This was perhaps the reason why, in the early 1950s, he deplored my agreement with the

Fund for the Republic, a project of the Ford Foundation, to write a history of the literary left. Newton must have had other reasons as well. It was no time to remind locals that one of them had contributed to magazines that were "soft on Communism" or to fuel the animus of the citizens who still blamed the college for keeping industry out of the city, ostensibly to safeguard what the *Daily Hampshire Gazette* once referred to as the annual crop of Smith College's "polished virginity." To these suspicious Northamptonians, Smith was not only a roosting place for liberals but hoity-toity as well; and, true enough, students and faculty sometimes acted as if they were a privileged autonomous power. Newton Arvin never did so, but in the end, his quiet self-effacement could not avert an unsought notoriety. He lived long enough to write an excellent book on Longfellow's life and work and to read Edmund Wilson's warm review of it in the *New Yorker,* but not long enough to shrug off the burden of his woes.

By the time Arvin died of pancreatic cancer in 1963, seven years after his trial and sentencing, Sergeant Regan's antiporn express had been shunted off to a quiet siding. During the previous six months, in faraway Poland, I had been getting detailed bulletins on Arvin's condition from Al Fisher. Over the years, one or both of us had been on hand to pick him up after one of his periodic collapses. This time, there was no recovery, although Arvin did manage to suffer less damage than did his younger companions caught in Regan's web with no phalanx of eminent friends to befriend them or to defray their legal expenses.

Newton Arvin's death came close to the end of my tenure at Smith. He had been one of the inducements for my going there as well as for my staying there, not simply because he taught me so much, but because I saw him as a guide to an authentic American culture that blended his birthplace of Valparaiso, Indiana, with Cambridge, Massachusetts, where he spent four years at Harvard College. It pleased me to learn that his grandfather, after shaking hands with President Grant in the Valparaiso railroad yards, had noted in his diary, "It done us all good." And it was reassuring that my timid friend and model Americanist was so enamored of the trans-American world that he had traveled through without ever crossing the Atlantic. When, after the war, I wrote to him from foreign parts, I always felt that our positions ought to have been reversed, that it was he who should have been sending me his impressions of Austria, Finland, Poland, Germany, England.

PART FOUR

I

In Northampton, a few years before the Japanese attack on Pearl Harbor, I had watched the war from a distance through the eyes of friends who were in it. My Harvard roommate, John Finch, now an intelligence officer on an airplane carrier, summed it up to me as "sand in your ears and stabrin pills and no toilet paper" and "an almost total dearth of good conversation." Just the same, he couldn't suppress his elation at being an actor in such a grand production. Envying him, I consoled myself with the likelihood that I, too, would soon be slotted for active service—that is, until it finally came home to me that I could very well be stuck where I was for the duration, barred from the privileged discourse of veterans and from the sacred precincts of overseas.

Nathaniel Hawthorne once impatiently asked if there were any corner of America where the "damned shadow" of Europe hadn't fallen. I relished that "shadow" and yearned for the lands that cast it, but Hitler would have to die in his bunker and Japan would surrender before I at last reached the magical place. Meanwhile I had been teaching in western Massachusetts with no expectations that the newly instituted Harvard degree in American civilization would shortly be my ticket to foreign lands I had given up hope of ever seeing. Only as the cold war widened and deepened did it occur to me that unintentionally I may have been preparing myself for some low-grade ambassadorial role. In the next twenty years, I taught and lectured for lengthy periods in

Austria, Finland, Poland, and England and for shorter stints in a half-dozen other countries. I went to these places not to "sell" the USA but to "explain" it, not to palliate its blemishes but to contextualize them. All the same, I pondered the ambiguities of my position as a cultural explicator of my country: to sing of its rocks and rills and templed hills (which I gladly did) and to air its dirty linen. Before the discovery of my newfound land, American history and literature had seemed to me a little schoolbookish and Longfellowish and too unmysterious to be interesting, whereas the words *Europe* and *abroad* conjured up childhood fantasies of an ancient and mysterious world. Natural timidity and a late Victorian upbringing kept me close to the safe and sane but left my imagination free to range, and throughout my program of Americanization, Europe was a dangerously attractive elsewhere. Moving from California to the Midwest and from there to New England, I had traveled the "course of empire" in reverse. Now I was ready to annex trans-America and to make it a part of my itinerary.

My first European landfall came in the summer of 1949, when I was one of eleven academics invited to teach in a summer session of the Salzburg Seminar in American Studies. Then in its third year, this still shaky operation had sprung from the impulse of an Austrian-born Harvard graduate student, Clemens Heller. Although loosely affiliated with international student groups, it was and remained for some time an essentially Harvard enterprise devoted to bringing the political, economic, and cultural history of the United States to young Europeans.

In Paris, I touched base with a few polyglot Smith colleagues and with Newton Arvin's friend and frequent Northampton visitor Truman Capote. Unlike me, Truman was not at all embarrassed by his linguistic poverty. In Milan, he told me, he had hailed a taxi driver with the cry of "Stoppo!" Truman fit comfortably into the ambience of the bar-restaurant Le Boeuf sur le Toit, where he took me to see Cocteau's murals and to watch handsome young men, all of them dressed in sober flannel suits and with identical coiffures, quietly sipping brandies with their Argentine patrons. He appeared to know all about the sensational careers of some of these look-alikes, as he did about the personal and public lives of their literary contemporaries.

A few days before I left Paris for Salzburg, Truman introduced me to "Nelly" Aspinwall-Bradley, his editor at Gallimard, a thin woman mannishly dressed, her face half-veiled. She told me that, when she was a child, Anatole France took her on walks and (if I remember correctly) she had known Proust. We drank very dry sherry in a high-ceilinged room elegantly underfurnished and richly bare. From her place on the Quai de Bethune, we strolled to a small restaurant where we joined Richard Wright and his wife. He had quit the States, he told me, to spare his half-white children from wounding racial incidents. He was a big, filled-out, relaxed man. His laugh was loud and warm. His suit jacket hung on the back of his chair. Wright talked at length on the Parisian literary scene (he was then in thick with the existentialists), but I missed most of what he was saying because I was listening to my hostess reminisce about Edith Wharton and André Gide.

In Salzburg, I lived for the next six weeks in a rather grand room in Schloss Leopoldskron, a run-down but still elegant eighteenth-century rococo castle once the residence of the impresario Max Reinhardt. That summer, it housed more than sixty young men and women, some of whom had been shooting at each other's compatriots a few years before. Not surprisingly, the atmosphere was at first a little tense. A Dutchman whose teeth had been knocked out by a guard in a Helgoland prison found it hard to sleep in the same room with Germans. A mild Danish economist told me quite matter-of-factly how he had disarmed and shot a Gestapo officer in a Copenhagen nightclub amid the schnapps and sandwiches. A young Austrian led a small party of his fellow seminarians—mostly Norwegian, but with a smattering from other countries—on a hike up the Untersberg, a modest mountain of some two thousand or so meters that rose abruptly from the Salzburg plain. Few of the company had ever done any climbing or had the right gear for it, but it was reckoned an easy jaunt, and all went well until the mischievous guide stranded his comrades, me included, in a spot where the slightest slip touched off cascades of rock. From there, he bounded off like a chamois, leaving us to find our way to the base as best we could. Rebuked by the seminar director and fearing expulsion, he apologized impenitently for his prank and assured me solemnly at the end of our session that the episode would prove to be a useful lesson for him, saying: "We Germans must learn tolerance. We must compel people to be tolerant."

It took a little time for some of the seminarians to harness their hatreds and more time to expunge them. The process was hastened by a providential case of scarlet fever early in the session that clapped the seminar in quarantine for over a week. Enforced propinquity helped to erode old suspicions and biases. Having a general topic to discuss—in sum, the history, institutions, and culture of the United States—may also have contributed to the ecumenical spirit. It gave the polynationalists—restrained, no doubt, from looking too closely at the horse's mouth—an excuse to test their shared assumptions about America and Americans. The seminar welded friendships and probably modified a few stereotypical prejudices about American culture; I doubt that it altered fixed convictions. Most of the students liked us and believed our good intentions. They also believed, or so it seemed to me then, that Americans—to be sure with notable exceptions—were naive, simple, and transparent. We were easy to please, and we smiled too much.

That summer, the Euro-American dialogue went on all day and into the night, the Europeans curious about the country from which they had been shut out for a decade, the Americans ever-ready to take up the touchiest issues and to dispute popular notions, pro and con, about the States. It was understood that our audience of incubating writers, artists, teachers, and public servants had been selected as future leaders in their respective countries and as the beneficiaries of our wisdom, but we ourselves would have been appalled had we been pegged as "cultural imperialists," a term not yet in the nomenclature of international debate. Instead, we strove to present an unvarnished America—to point out conscientiously its unresolved problems of race and class (the issue of gender had yet to surface in such circles) and to explode the myth of American innocence.

Contradictions between theory and practice were strikingly evident in Salzburg itself, where a body of African-American soldiers, yet to be integrated into white units, gave the seminarians an instructive look at Jim Crow. The American military had granted the seminar access to the GI buses running between central Salzburg and its environs. The African-American soldiers we encountered on these buses ostentatiously fondled their blond Austrian girlfriends while flashing us a look that said, "What do you white bastards think of this?" Our students observed these and comparable scenes with great interest and plied us with questions about lynchings and other violations of the democratic credo. I couldn't tell whether their fascination with American violence was inspired by social concern or by an impulse to puncture American triumphalism.

The next four seminar sessions I attended (in 1954, 1956, 1957, and 1965) were at once different and similar, with the same Schloss Leopoldskron but better living arrangements: the tap water was drinkable, the fare less Spartan. In the space of seven years, the charming and mercenary city had very nearly painted over its National Socialist colors. Salzburg merchants, exploiting the Mozart logo, coined money, while in cheerful cafés and *Bierstuben*, nostalgic Salzburgians relived glory days in occupied Holland, Denmark, and Norway. More than a trace of the city's greed and inhumanity festered under its pastry carapace. Before the Anschluss, a Smith College colleague, the musicologist Alfred Einstein, had covered the Salzburg musical scene for the *Berliner Tageblatt*. His horrendous account of those days suffused beautiful Salzburg in a poisonous glow that I was never quite able to dispel in subsequent visits.

In 1956, I organized a session on writing and publishing in American society. I can no longer remember what I had in mind when I proposed it. It was held at a moment when European students were no longer finding American popular culture so novel as it had seemed to them when the seminar was new and the United States less accessible. Of the four faculty members, I was the only bona fide academic. Two were freelance journalists and social commentators, the third an unaffiliated economic historian and a specialist on the publishing industry. All of them were unprofessorial in speech and demeanor and decidedly unboosterish. A Scots participant wondered at the end of our session if the lecturers hadn't been a little overcritical of American pastimes and institutions, especially Dwight Macdonald, whose "highly subjective approach" and "pronounced views" on American mass culture offended, delighted, or puzzled his listeners. Certainly their professors in Helsinki, Oslo, Paris, Mannheim, Berlin, and Aarhus didn't argue unceremoniously with their students, and if those professors had chosen to lecture on the cultural implications of packaging consumer goods in America, they probably would not have likened the difficulty of unwrapping a bar of soap or chocolate to that of undressing a woman. Professor Macdonald, they concluded, was "unacademic" but "stimulating."

After 1956, the sessions gradually shrunk from four weeks to two or fewer, and such mavericks as Dwight Macdonald were soon out of sync with the seminar's increasingly corporate and political image. The gradual displacement of enthusiastical types kept it from going under, as it surely would have done without the intervention of practical administrators and infusions of cash. It broadened its scope, sharpened its focus, and enhanced the role of business and social sciences. Something engagingly amateurish disappeared in the process, an atmosphere and spontaneity epitomized for me in the music and words of the *Threepenny Opera* (whose score we memorized in the summer of 1949) and in the recordings of Duke Ellington, Count Basie, and Louis Armstrong that I had brought from Paris.

Years later, Armstrong announced that he was taking his band to Moscow "to bruise those cats with happy music." In a less stunning way, that was what we were hoping to do in Austria, taking care not to omit the blue notes and minor chords. Lest we appear like happy Americans unscathed by life, we feigned a cosmopolitanism we hadn't earned and avoided any appearance of trying to "win friends and influence people." Ten years later, with the cold war welling up, it had become pretty obvious that American "representatives" abroad were expected as a matter of course to do precisely that.

II

I had come to Helsinki as a visiting professor in the early fall of 1951, just when the local Communist press was fulminating against Tito and Titoism and providing graphic proof (pictures of insectivores crawling out of canisters) of American germ warfare in Korea. Finland's ragged collaboration with the Germans (from 1941 to 1944) after its defeat by the USSR in the Winter War had tarnished its luster, but most Americans sided with "brave little Finland"—the only country to honor its World War I debts—without caring very much about its recent history. My fancied Finland was a pastiche of legends and tall tales. It connoted Ultima Thule, the brooding music of Sibelius, Lapps and reindeer, the Olympic long-distance runner Paavo Nurmi.

What I saw and heard between September 1951 and May of the next year evaporated the last remnants of my illusions about the "great Soviet experiment." This was not a sudden illumination, nor did it mark a violent turnabout in my politics. I simply began to see the Finns as a stubborn people who had good reason to resent their conquerors. I empathized with the taxi drivers who spat when they drove past the ugly Soviet embassy (paid for by the

Finns) that stood out like a fist in the center of a battered city, and I empathized with Finnish veterans aged sixteen to sixty missing legs, arms, hands, fingers; one met them everywhere. The Mannerheim Line, touted in the American press as another Maginot Line, proved to have been little more than a series of pillboxes strung across the Karelian Isthmus. Baron Mannerheim, the "notorious butcher" of Communist propaganda, changed from a cartoon figure into a hero and a noble man. Reading his remarkable memoir conveyed to me a measure of his stature, as did my conversation with the physician who had accompanied him on an official visit to what he called Hermann Goering's "castle." The physician told me of the general's icy correctness as he negotiated with men he considered scum and of an occasion when the general had ordered his staff to pay a formal courtesy call on Helsinki's chief rabbi after the Germans had requested a list of the city's Jews.

Ostensibly, I was taking part in a cultural exchange program between the United States and other nations. My business in Helsinki was primarily to teach American literature, but visiting scholars were also expected to dispense "American culture" in all of its ramifications—to "explain" the USA and to mollify anti-American biases. We probably made some of those we reached think better of Americans and confirmed the opinions of others that the United States had no culture that Europeans need take very seriously, that America was rich and powerful but unlettered and parochial.

Such views were much less prevalent in Finland than elsewhere in Western Europe, where British English had a higher cachet than demotic American. My Finnish students hadn't had the opportunities to study English available to their Swedish, Norwegian, or Danish peers; besides, they were passionately nationalistic. Most of them had enrolled in the American literature class simply to fulfill a requirement, and they didn't consider American professors the real McCoy anyway. Some may have thought me less solemn and authoritarian than their teachers trained in the German tradition, who expected students to rise when a professor entered the classroom and to wait for the professor's nod to be seated.

Exchanges were easier in the discussions that followed my lectures at the United States Information Agency or after my impromptu talks to miscellaneous audiences in which I held forth without qualms on all things American. Once I spoke on American humor, using *New Yorker* cartoons as illustrations. My listeners sat silent and puzzled until the point of a graphic joke suddenly detonated. I lectured on racial discrimination in the United States and disputed the claim of a team from the State Department, including two African-Americans, that the problem was being resolved. I ridiculed the silly folklore about student life in American universities, only to find it embalmed (to the vast amusement of my audience) in a USIA documentary film that followed my remarks: in one episode, a young nerd learns that too much study diminishes the spirit and that going to basketball games with friends can make you human.

All that year, I steeped myself in Finnish lore and culture. I read Finland's epic poem *Kalevala* and Alexis Kivi's *The Seven Brothers*, frequented the folk museum, and heard more opera than I ever heard again, the choruses singing in Finnish, the soloists in their respective tongues. I sampled the movies (most of them geared to rural tastes) without comprehension. In a Helsinki nightclub, I contrasted the indifference of the male patrons to naked chorus girls with their huge delight in stand-up comedians. I became a sauna addict just to experience twice a week the sensation of physical-spiritual cleansing after the purgatorial heat. I watched small boys learning to skate in the icy cold and listened to their stern papas order them to get up and stop whimpering after a tumble. At noontime on Saturdays, workmen congregated around a government liquor dispensary not far from my house in the University Botanical Garden and emerged with satchels of fortified brandy they immediately opened after stepping out into the street. By early afternoon, bodies were toppling in the city parks.

Throughout my ten months in Helsinki, I felt the proximity of Leningrad and grew accustomed to the Russian voices I heard every day on the radio. One program beamed from Moscow opened with an ominous musical passage and the words, announced in sepulchral tones, "The Dollar Shadow Over Europe." I had learned just enough Russian by this time to exchange pleasantries and to carry on simple conversations. The next step was to try my rudimentary skills in Russia itself. A foreign service officer passing through the Helsinki gateway had offered to put me up in the American embassy in Moscow if I could wangle a visa. I paid a visit to the Soviet consulate to get one, because I felt I owed myself a trip after daily struggles with Russian verbs and my laborious efforts to translate Soviet polemics against American cannibals, butchers, pigs, and maniacs. While my application was pending, I met F. A. Garanin, first secretary of the Soviet embassy, at the house of the American press attaché, who, knowing my problem, had invited him to dinner as a possible facilitator. He came alone, explaining that his wife was ill. Nothing out of the way happened that night except Garanin's request to see a sensational issue of *Collier's*, an American weekly that had just published a fictional piece prefiguring the invasion of the Soviet Union by the United States. After flicking through it and clucking his tongue, Garanin gravely declared that the State Department was concocting such a war. We fervently demurred, and Garanin proposed a toast: "Down with warmongers." We drank to that.

A few days later, Garanin sent us tickets to a road show of Soviet entertainers at the exhibition hall off of Union Street. The program turned out to be varied and splashy. I very much enjoyed the twenty-two pretty girls shrieking with mock joy as they whirled in perfect coordination, the balalaika players and acrobats and folksy singers and dancers. Especially memorable was a thin Buster Keatonish sleight-of-hand artist as quiet and subtle as the others were noisy. Garanin, who met us, as planned, during intermission, asked me to dinner on the following Thursday. Pressing business forced him to cancel that appointment, but a few days later, he set up a lunch at the Royal Restaurant adjoining the Swedish Theater, where I had recently enjoyed a performance of Gogol's *Revizor* and where, a year earlier, the atomic physicist Bruno Pontecorvo was last seen before his disappearance. We left the restaurant thoroughly soused three and a half hours later and parted at a busy intersection.

Garanin had an agenda. The purpose of the lunch was to convince me that the United States was waging bacteriological warfare in Korea; that the future lay with men like himself who were flourishing in a vital society; that in America, a bitterly unhappy working class suffered cruel exploitations; that Garanin's prospects were bright whereas mine were not (he had lived in America and knew how ground down schoolteachers were); and that I would have no problem obtaining a visa if I signed a statement for the magazine *Ogenek* that Americans were resorting to germ warfare. (He had positive proof that they were.) Convinced, after much fencing, that I thought his allegations nonsense, he no longer bothered to hide his irritation with America and with me: President Truman was nothing but a "haberdasher"; I was a "cosmopolitan," Garanin's euphemism for a "rootless Jew." "Let's tell our bosses that we talked about literature," he suggested at the end of our boozy conversation. "You do that," I said, adding, "I don't have to report to anyone." Nor did I until several weeks later, when I happened to mention my drunken tête-à-tête to a friend in the American legation. Stunned by my negligence, he advised me to speak to a colleague of his concerned with such matters, and that person told me of Garanin's recruiting activities. Helsinki, a junction for westerners entering and leaving the Soviet Union in the 1950s, had also been good hunting ground for Soviet agents, a fact I hadn't appreciated until my run-in with the first secretary. A decade later, in Poland, the seduction of American foreign service officers had become a topic of more than hypothetical interest.

John Fitzgerald Kennedy was the only American president I ever thought of as "my president." Until he was elected in 1960, his predecessors since Wilson had been "old men." He was five years my junior, the first and last president whose political career I followed from its incubation to its abrupt end, and the only one about whom I had some personal knowledge. I graded his so-so examination paper for a Harvard American literature course, and I later supported his senatorial campaign in Massachusetts, as one of the "Professors for Kennedy." At my request, he helped secure the naturalization of a Smith colleague (a Goya specialist and former member of the Spanish Loyalist government) and kept me informed of his efforts. We once gossiped about our mutual Harvards, during a lunch that followed his engagingly delivered commencement address to Smith College seniors. A smart speechwriter had laced the talk with apposite quotations from Donne, Blake, and Yeats, exemplary poets for the New Critics and their Smith disciples. Thereafter, whatever I learned of the White House and its inmates came from the novelist (and favorite of the Kennedy clan) Edwin O'Connor and from JFK's staff member Arthur M. Schlesinger Jr.

Any active Democrat in Massachusetts at this time was likely to end up willy-nilly in the Kennedy camp, but I didn't consider myself a Kennedy henchman. Purportedly, JFK's father was odious. JFK's brother Robert, whose politically motivated and troublesome junket to Warsaw I had heard about just after I got there, was said to be ruthless and arrogant, and his associations with Senator Joseph McCarthy, however brief, were a black mark. JFK's brother Ted, whom I had sized up as a spoiled youth when I was introduced to him at a Democratic Party gathering, proved to be even more unlikable while recovering in Northampton's Cooley-Dickinson Hospital after a plane crash. He behaved so outrageously, I was told by the orthopedist who treated him, that his old family nurse was summoned from Boston to curb him. This was well before his translation into an effective Senate leader and perhaps the most politically constructive and statesmanlike of the Kennedy brothers.

By the mid-1950s, I thought better of the Kennedys, cheered

by JFK's geniality and wit when he spoke on that graduation day and firmly in his corner when he debated a rebarbative Richard Nixon on television. Yet I still had mixed feelings about the Kennedys. Given the disparities between their public and private behavior and their questionable friendships, how could one determine what they stood for? Where did one place them in the political spectrum? They hankered for power (they had all the money they needed), behaved at times like a well-heeled clutch of Snopes, and for years tried without notable success to keep their private affairs private. The president managed to take his pleasures relatively free from public scrutiny, and the Kennedy political machine, from my perspective, operated smoothly and efficiently.

Scuttlebutt about the president's extramarital amours was common, according to the indefatigable diary keeper Arthur Inman, who was wondering as early as November 1963 what future historians would make of them. "Of course," Inman added, "this side of a man's life is his own business but is, in final analysis, a part of his record as a man if true." Inman was pondering "St. Kennedy" and his "canonization" only a few months before he shot himself on the same day that Jack Ruby shot Lee Harvey Oswald in a Dallas jail.

As it turned out, in our national history, Inman's "St. Kennedy" has overshadowed, if not entirely extinguished, Kennedy the libertine. JFK and his wife were the first White House occupants—save for Theodore Roosevelt, whose cultural interests were more authentic and various than JFK's—to create a semblance of a court where artists, writers, intellectuals, and entertainers could gather and glitter. The charming presidential couple transformed Eisenhower's capitol, it was said, into a swinging Camelot. Prominent people welcomed invitations to their assemblages of deep thinkers, wits, entertainers, and beautiful women. Norman Mailer wrote of his spiritual kinship with "Jackie" Kennedy and fancied himself a hip Aristotle to Kennedy's Alexander. In fact, the president dazzled his ad hoc courtiers far more than they beguiled him. A passage from Emerson's *The Conduct of Life* might have served as his epitaph:

"The finished man of the world must eat of every apple once. He must hold his hatreds at arm's length, and not remember spite. He has neither friends nor enemies, but values men only as channels of power." ❦

Shortly before I got to Warsaw in September 1962, the Polish security police had photographed a member of the American embassy in bed with a Polish woman. Terrified lest his wife be shown visible proof of his marital betrayal, he elected to betray his country and turn over to his blackmailers the master plan of American sub-rosa activities in Poland for that year. I learned of this caper after my arrival. I had been warned of tapped telephones, bugged apartments, and beautiful ladies knocking on doors after midnight, but I didn't put much stock in these tales. Later, I recalled the State Department man in Washington who dryly remarked to me that while he couldn't advise me what to do if I were asked to be a spy (he didn't say by whom), he merely hoped that I would refuse.

My picture of Poland had been compounded from a mix of fact, fiction, and imagination. A large number of my fellow citizens in Northampton, Massachusetts, as I've said, were the children and grandchildren of Polish immigrants, and Galician Polish could be heard on Main Street and in the fields and orchards east of the Connecticut River where, for several summers, I had suckered tobacco plants, weeded onions, cut asparagus, and harvested apples for Polish-American farmers. But Poland was for me a phantasmagorical map dotted with unpronounceable names, a blood-drenched land in the Eastern fens, comprised of dark forests, fields of sugar beets, burning ghettos, and obscene encampments stacked with human hair and children's shoes. I had chosen Poland over Hawaii (where I had also been invited), because my visa to Russia never came while I was in Finland, and

I wanted to know what it was like to live in a Communist society. Warsaw lacked palm trees, but it was said to be au courant. Polish movies were in vogue. Friends returning from brief visits spoke enthusiastically of the Warsaw scene, of sopping up vodka and gossip at the bar of the Bristol Hotel with avant-garde artists and intellectuals.

On my first day in Warsaw, I scouted for a corkscrew *(korkociag)* and learned to ask for one in Polish: it took me a few months to pick up enough of the language to ask directions or to notify the person jammed up against me on a packed bus that I was getting off at the next stop. In time, I managed to puzzle out stories and articles with help from friends, to travel on trains and planes with confidence, and to chat haltingly in a goulash of Russian, Polish, German, and French, but I quickly gave up the ridiculous notion of becoming a specialist of the New Poland. It was enough to make the most of my student contacts and professional associates, to brush against principled and unprincipled oppositionists, the *combinators* (wheelers and dealers), the old gentry and hoi polloi. Compounding the often tendentious and contradictory opinions of my informants, I fearlessly generalized on Poland and the Polish character. Polish men, I observed, were often proud, quixotic, and grandiose. They made lousy Communists and adored their charming and resourceful women. The social machinery of the country was a clanky amalgam of the old Central European and more recent Stalinist bureaucracy. I noted the surface tranquility of daily life, the absence of any egregious signs of the police state (save perhaps the unnatty militia toting tommy guns), and the way average citizens steeled themselves against the expected insolence or indifference of officialdom.

In Warsaw, I became friends again with Ambassador John Moors Cabot, minister to Finland, who had been my sometime tennis partner during my stay there. Now, ten years later, he occupied a dicier post at a dicier moment. One Sunday morning, we drove to a small forest preserve crisscrossed with paths and walked his two dogs for several hours. It was the only piece of Poland nearby where he and his wife could talk without the risk of being bugged. The ambassador described himself as a Republican in his heart and a Democrat in his head. He talked about Finland (a country he loved), Latin America (which he knew very well), and Massachusetts politics. But the crisis bubbling in Cuba preoccupied him at the moment. It crested one month later, on the night of October 25, as Russian cargo vessels approached the American warships blockading the Cuban coast. That night, a tense embassy hosted a dinner I won't forget. The Polish government had been soft-pedaling alarms that could have provoked hoarding, bank withdrawals, and raids on stores. President Kennedy's "quarantine" of Cuba, according to the Communist press, was a cynical move to ensure his election, but it could turn ugly if the Soviet Union decided to resist American "banditry." We nervously waited for the news of the negotiations between the United States and the USSR. Would the Polish foreign minister and his staff show up? Their presence or absence would be a telltale indicator. They did appear—with beaming faces—and everyone relaxed.

Surveying the exhibit of contemporary American painting and sculpture on display in the embassy, Poland's witty foreign minister recalled an exchange he'd been privy to in 1952 between A. Y. Vyshinsky, Stalin's foreign minister, and the U.S. ambassador to the United Nations. The point at issue was a painting by Fernand Léger. The former declared it a decadent modernist botch, the latter an emblem of America's enterprising spirit. On being told that Léger was a member of the French Communist Party, both art experts found reasons to reverse their initial judgments. The Poles didn't take the cold war casually (their country, after all, was a kind of buffer zone), but the ironists among them saw its Tweedledee-Tweedledum implications. A Krakow historian in Moscow during the Cuban crisis told me that the Muscovites he talked to on the subway trains were much too absorbed in the plight of a nice Russian girl reported to be immured against her will in an Arabian harem (and too incensed against her

"African" husband) to worry about the Soviet-American confrontation—an instance of poppycock triumphant over facts.

Between Khrushchev's revelations at the Twentieth Congress
of the Communist Party of the Soviet Union in 1956 and the
Cuban crisis six years later, the USSR's grip on its satellites had
publicly loosened. For example, scholarly books and articles published in Poland (it made no difference what the subject) no
longer required a fulsome acknowledgment to the omniscient
Stalin. A mistake didn't inevitably cost a scholar his job or a
chance to travel outside the country. There were moments when I
had to keep reminding myself that I was living in a police state,
that I wasn't so unsupervised as I fancied myself to be, and that
there was no guarantee that Stalinism was kaput. I made sure that
nothing substantively political colored my lectures, but I gave no
thought to what I may have conveyed through tone and indirec-
tion until I heard Erskine Caldwell's rambling talk. Tall and
bleak, his face looking as if it had been cut out of wood, he warned
me that he was "an authority on only one thing, myself," a remark
I quoted when I introduced him. The students liked his quirky,
off-the-cuff answers to their questions. This American writer had
started out as an economist and sociologist, had learned little from
critics, and had found small profit in the fiction of his peers
(Faulkner excepted). The only book that interested him was the
one he happened to be writing. I observed without astonishment
that the students acclaimed him and snubbed the lecture that followed his, a red-carpet event to which the entire English department had been summoned. The designated audience listened
politely and unresponsively to the speaker, a handsome young
professor from Humboldt University in East Berlin, who summed
up contemporary American literature as an overview of a brutal
degenerate society.

Usually, I tried to avoid gatherings of this kind. I looked for
venues into which one could disappear at will, my favorite hideout
being the Palace of Culture, Joseph Stalin's present to the Poles.
Set off from Aleje Jerozolimskie by a cobblestone square, it

housed rooms and halls and monolithic corridors, a theater, a swimming pool I heard about but never saw, and enclaves for exhibits and displays. My beat, on floor 6, was the library and reading room of the Polish Academy of Science, where I often conferred with one of its librarians—I called him Captain Nemo—who for many years had been working on a project to simplify the Chinese alphabet. When we became better acquainted, we engaged in a benign humanist conspiracy, which was nothing less than to smuggle books into the academy's shelves, books to challenge the idolatries of both Left and Right. Captain Nemo, a religious man and something of a mystic, referred to them as "Eternals." I thought of them as time bombs that would spread what Henry James called "the virus of suggestion." Ours wasn't a plot to undermine the government but, rather, a learning experiment, a scheme to plant a cache of books for anglophone readers on subjects the authorities deemed irrelevant or subversive.

With the help of an American cultural officer, I did manage to deliver a few batches of Captain Nemo's "Eternals," but no medicine for his country's ethnic and religious ailments. Officially, anti-Semitism was illegal in Poland, but it didn't take much poking around to discover that it was thriving everywhere in the country. The reasons, as they were explained to me, were because the Jews who returned to Poland after the war were Stalinists and remained Stalinists; because Jews dominated journalism and other communication channels in Poland; because, despite their ostensible Polishness and the difficulty of spotting a Jew who had "passed" for Polish, Jews remained spiritually alien in Poland; and because the proliferation of big noses, big ears, and kinky hair would uglify the Polish countenance. The last explanation was said to me by a learned man who assured me that little would be left of Polish literature were the Jews eliminated, that middle-class Polish families had Jewish connections, and that every Pole had his pet Jew. Shortly after our talk, I visited Oświęcim (Auschwitz) and wrote in my journal (May 1963):

Atrocities cleaned up and classified. We stroll through one of the wooden buildings and peer at glassed-in bins piled high with suitcases bearing the names of their incinerated owners. We see the trolleys that trundled corpses into the ovens. No indication here that most of the fire fodder were Jews, but photographs of Polish martyrs hang here and there. A holiday atmosphere. Busloads of children chatter on the grassy turf. The tidied camp looks almost festive. Flags and ice cream.

In Poland, as in Austria and Finland, I kept my remarks free of anything hinting at the "great struggle being waged between two opposing ways of life." On the contrary, I considered it almost obligatory to acknowledge America's national blemishes and unfulfilled goals, on the principle that one served one's country best by responsibly criticizing it. Polish security officials took for granted that foreign scholars were putative spies—an assumption not all that far-fetched when you come to think of it. An American of romantic disposition living behind the iron curtain might fancy himself a Yankee version of Rudyard Kipling's Kim (Kimball O'Hara), secret agent of the Raj, and a player in the great international game. But it never crossed my mind, as I was leaving Warsaw for home in the early summer of 1963, that my telephone conversations with a Polish acquaintance—a Communist Party member, no less—might have been monitored or that one of the charges brought against him four years later would be his frequent "contacts" with me. If it had crossed my mind, I should have been less skeptical about Polish efficiency and readier to believe that a country where the elevators and the heating and plumbing were unreliable might still possess a state-of-the-art surveillance system.

I returned to Poland the next summer, this time to Krakow, but not before being yanked off the train at Frankfort am Oder by the East German police and detained for half a day for want of a proper visa. Two subjects then preoccupied my Polish friends. The first was the Kennedy assassination. Whatever their politics, all of the Poles I spoke to "knew" that the president had not been murdered by a single assassin. They did not believe for a minute that his death and its weird aftermath were merely coincidental. They deduced as much from rumor and gossip and from the low-down provided by inside dopesters undeceived by official explanations. The second and even more distressing subject on their minds was the nomination of Barry Goldwater as the Republican Party's presidential candidate. This "calamity" turned some of the best-informed and most well-balanced Poles into Chicken Littles and inspired fearful prophecies. A Goldwater victory would strengthen the pro-Chinese wing in the Eastern Bloc and further snarl the Sino-Russian imbroglio. It would give credence to Gomułka's fantasy that linked Senator Goldwater, whom he condemned, to revanchist Germans. Should Goldwater win the national election (and my friends believed he well might), another war was not unthinkable. During the Cuban missile crisis, Kennedy and Khrushchev had been able to talk with each other over the head of the paranoid Castro. Now imagine the outcome if Goldwater were elected president and decided to invade Cuba.

I had marched under JFK's flag as a skeptical volunteer, more at odds with his haters than enamored of him. I did not subscribe to the conspiracy theories that continued to flourish long after his assassination. Where and when he was killed, however, did encourage baleful fantasies, like my response to the Republican convention in San Francisco in July 1964, which nominated Barry Goldwater. Perhaps, I speculated in my journal, the nomination signaled a new era, not immediately (for I thought the Goldwaterites would be smashed in the next election), but in a discernible future. From my parochial perspective, the mean-faced people screaming, "Barry, Barry, we want Barry," and the Goldwater partisans well distributed west of the Mississippi constituted a new class, suspicious of Washington and especially distrustful of the metropolitan East. What exactly they were for was harder to pin down than what they were against. It took me some time before I was able to distinguish the blunt Arizona senator from his claque of passionate evangelicals, ignorant of history and contemptuous of war. I believed that Texas was the power center of his movement and read the Goldwater debacle as a paragraph in the history of a Southwest imperium, government within a government.

Henry Nash Smith from Dallas—a fellow guinea pig in the first few years of Harvard's American civilization program and a cherished friend and instructor—had taught me to identify a "good Texan" and a "bad Texan." "Bad Texans" included demagogic politicians who raised the slush funds to retain the infamous oil depletion allowance, as well as the regents of the University of Texas who saw to it that subversive books, for example, John Dos Passos's *The Big Money,* were kept out of Texas classrooms. Among the "good Texans" were homegrown mavericks, Rooseveltian liberals, and readers of the *Texas Observer* who thought the way we did.

In Austin several decades later, I met the writer James Michener, whom I described in my journal as "heavy and thickset" and "on the tallish side," with a "rough square face." I wrote that he was "not a finely tuned instrument but a kind of traveling reporter who has made long stays in various parts of the world and sopped up reams of information that he periodically disgorges in novels-cum-travel books." I further observed: "He relies on his eyes, of course, but also on a corps of informants and fact gatherers. Now his subject is Texas and Austin his base while he gathers materials on this fabulous state." Michener told me of invitations pouring in from rich men who offered him their private planes to take him wherever he wanted to go. He had been asked to speak, to give interviews, to attend gigantic festivities, the details of which—even when soberly described—are too bizarre and extravagant to be believed. These Texas moguls, he said, held parties for five thousand guests. They imported whole orchestras, bought every rose in the state for special occasions, rented circuses, built medieval castles on the plains. These friendly, kind, and generous folk loved guns and horses. They also loved Michener, and he liked them.

Of all the presidentiads I lived through and studied, the most primed for tragedy seemed to me that of Lyndon Baines Johnson. Like Faulkner's Thomas Sutpen (in *Absalom, Absalom!*), LBJ was a powerful and potentially good man riddled with flaws, brought down by stubborn pride and blindness to portents. I imputed to LBJ a latent decency that mitigated his alleged brutality and grossness. Raised in the cockpit of Texas politics, he had learned how to persuade and to coerce when playing the rough political game. He was also, and I believe sincerely so, a legatee of FDR and closer than his master to the experiences of the poor and ground down, whose problems he felt obliged and competent to remedy. In 1963, I took for granted that LBJ was mostly on my side, and I kept a sneaking sympathy for him even after the debacle in Vietnam and the collapse of his "Great Society" program, when the literary intelligentsia were plunging their harpoons into his vulnerable flank.

But the war in Vietnam diverted him from his grand design and alienated his liberal constituency—myself included. I opposed the American "military mission" with the arguments that it was the wrong war, at the wrong time, in the wrong place. Like most Americans, I could not imagine its social consequences: that poor and uneducated boy-men would bear the brunt of it, that it would water the seeds of an impending drug culture, and that thousands of college-aged men would evade military action in Southeast Asia because they were politically and economically positioned to do so. Students and their teachers in the 1960s often faced "morally interesting situations" when a course grade might determine whether a student was drafted or deferred.

Why did such social technicians as McGeorge Bundy and Walt Whitman Rostow, men I knew and admired, lend their hearts and skills to this wretched business? Why did they accept so trustfully the mechanical domino theory preached by the secretary of state, John Foster Dulles? Why did the usually unflappable Bundy choke with fury (as once happened in my presence) when sharply questioned about his Vietnam role? What would he have thought of the two-volume collection of Vietnam War reportage in the Library of America—the publishing venture he did so much to make possible—that highlights the war's horror and futility?

On April 8, 1968, after his unctuous and irritating apologia about his intentions and accomplishments, President Johnson spoke to a national audience of his decision to halt the bombing of undefended Vietnam cities and to confine air attacks to military concentrations. Then, almost as an afterthought, he announced that he would not be a candidate for reelection. Many listeners, bored or disgusted, had already turned off their sets. Senator Fulbright thought LBJ hadn't gone far enough, that his gesture was likely to provoke Hanoi's anger and contempt. But Fulbright had to eat his words. Hanoi did reply, and the stock market zoomed up as Republican and Democratic politicians pondered the president's withdrawal.

Four days before the president redefined American military tactics in Vietnam, I wrote in my journal:

Thursday, Martin Luther King assassinated an earthshaking event, perhaps more profound in its implications than JFK's murder. What prompts the massive lamentation? Guilt, fear, compassion? A belated recognition that a saint has been living with us incognito? At this moment a funeral is being conducted in Atlanta. The vice president is there and the mayor and foreign diplomats and artists etc. etc. An extraordinary outpouring as if this man's death has shifted a huge weight and let loose a wave to wash away the offal of a nation. It feels as if America now is on a different tack. In Europe and elsewhere, these assassinations are seen as the acts of a deranged and vicious people. We seem to see them as inadvertent prods to virtue.

King's transfiguration coincided with LBJ's plummeting descent. LBJ quit his office a wounded titan, hurt and bewildered by his repudiation. I had only an inkling of the person in the towering frame whom I had once hailed and then turned against, but I still resented the smart-ass baiters who, when it was safe, mauled the dead lion. 🎗

I was out of Poland before Goldwater's political debacle, but the roiled connotations that thereafter accompanied references to "America" and, even more, to the smudged cliché of "the American dream" were objectified for me three years later during a month's stay in Uruguay. An invitation to lecture there had come from a friend recently installed in the Montevideo embassy whom I'd seen a lot of in Warsaw. Energetic, well trained, thoughtful, he had learned his job in the Soviet Union, Yugoslavia, and Poland and had grown impatient with the entrenched so-called Latin-American hands for whom any Uruguayan was a potential Communist and likely to be anti-American. He had come to believe that the best-known Uruguayan artists and intellectuals aligned in some fashion with the Left would welcome an outlet to the political center if they were offered one. Perhaps he thought my own well-publicized opposition to the Vietnam War and my recent stint at Warsaw University (1962–63) might make me seem less of a "cultural imperialist" in student eyes and might even circumvent the militant student minority that had shut down the university. Something of this was intimated to me by my State Department friend along with the hope that I would make useful contacts and investigate the possibilities of arousing interest in American studies.

I quickly adjusted to the routine of comfortable dilapidated Montevideo. Ancient Fords, Chevies, Dodges, Austens, Buicks, and De Sotos tooling down the boulevards gave the city in the summer of 1966 the look of a 1930s movie set. Everything about it appeared relaxed, not spick-and-span. Every building, wall, and tree was placarded with the slogans of rival political parties. The next four weeks were unremittingly busy. Almost every day, I'd find myself speaking to an organization or group, sometimes more than one, about things American. I seldom went to bed before four o'clock in the morning. My visit, someone told me, coincided with a reported rift between the political and cultural branches of the State Department. I was said to be a counteradministration representative sent down from Washington at a moment when the embassy was about to spell out the government's line on why we were in Vietnam. I don't know how this nonsense evolved, but one couldn't help noting the friction between the conservatives in the United States Information Agency and the gung ho political officers in Montevideo. Some of the former had opposed my coming. They considered me a crypto-Communist (if not the real article) and a loose cannon who would require constant monitoring. They worried that I'd make some horrendous gaffe in my television debut and be chewed up by student activists.

The first test came on a disagreeable August night at the University of the Republic. Sheets of rain were sweeping through the open stone galleries when I entered the building and found forty to fifty people waiting for me in the dank lecture room. In the outside hall, a cluster of pickets held signs inviting me to go home. Dead ringers for the earnest and unhandsome figures I had known and sometimes worked with in the 1930s, they were more glum than vehement. As I was about to begin my talk on William Faulkner, the lights went out but quickly were switched back on again. There were no further interruptions. The USIA people took a dark view of this "confrontation," unaware that an academic council with student representatives had arranged for my visit. The demonstration was the work of a small and unsupported splinter group. It did, however, have a productive and amusing aftermath, thanks largely to an alert and knowledgeable USIA officer, the antithesis of his elders. Among his many friends in the Uruguayan intelligentsia was the editor of *Marcha*, a prestigious political and literary journal unferociously anti-American and widely read in the Rio Plate area. My interview with this droll and sardonic journalist grew less formal the more we drank, so instead of doing a job on me, he proposed that he put questions to me and that I write out replies, which he would then print unaltered. One USIA officer, I learned later, pronounced *Marcha*'s offer an obvious trap and urged it to be rejected, but he was overruled by a higher authority who welcomed the chance to break out of a long-standing public relations stalemate.

The questions the editor of *Marcha* invited me to respond to amounted in substance to an ironical, if good-humored, critique of me in my role of cultural spokesman. They were intended to expose the contradictions of my pose as a self-styled liberal in disagreement with his country's policy in Vietnam yet lecturing to Uruguayans under the American aegis. The editor asked how I could reconcile this sponsorship with my convictions—whether I wasn't, at bottom, a "cultural imperialist." In my reply, I conceded that I was, but only if that term defines one who tries to make the best case he can for his country's values and culture. It didn't oblige me to defend what I disbelieved or opposed. Hence I and others could write or speak against the Vietnam War without fear of official censure. The State Department knew my views, but I was here in Uruguay as a student of literature, not as an international relations expert. Even so, that didn't prevent me from speaking freely on any subject that seemed pertinent to me. The journalist asked whether my presence was a form of "imperialist penetration," to which I responded that all books, lectures, concerts, exhibitions, ballets, and so forth "penetrate" in some measure. Should they be banned, I asked, for fear of ideological contamination? I emphasized that I had come to Uruguay to talk about North American literature, just as the Leningrad Philharmonic (then concertizing in Montevideo) had presumably come to play music.

This palaver sounds a little disingenuous to me now but did not then. The *Marcha* interview, sandwiched between a piece on a Chinese general and a condemnation of Pablo Neruda for accepting an award from the Rockefeller Foundation in New York, amounted to a seal of approval. Student groups now sought me out, picked me up, and spirited me away to private conclaves where they poured out their discontents. Defiantly on the Left, hostile to their increasingly militarist government, and yet unaware that their anti-Americanism might be in part a cover for their own personal disappointments, they looked for and found a pervasive American presence in the Uruguayan oligarchy, in the press, and (not least) in the mechanisms of cultural exchange. At the same time, they acted like aggrieved children who had been abandoned by their rich Uncle Sam. I did my best to dissipate the myths, pro and con, about the United States. I possibly changed a few minds or served as a vent for the anger and frustration of some young Uruguayans.

I left Montevideo knowing little more about the country and people than I had before I came. I completely failed to detect the signs of the incubating Tupamar violence and the end of civilian government. I was not as confident in 1966 as I had been in 1949, my first experience abroad, of my ability to "explain" the complicated and contradictory USA. "My country, right or wrong," declared Stephen Decatur, naval hero of the Tripolitan and 1812 wars and known "for his reckless and stubborn patriotism." Col. Robert McCormick, publisher of the *Chicago Tribune,* carried Decatur's credo on the masthead of his paper, but what would Emerson have thought about an enterprise to market American civilization or of becoming, however inadvertently, the coadjutor of hucksters? That question troubled me a little, whereas I found it easy and congenial to line up with artists and intellectuals at once avant-garde and politically liberal and opposed, admittedly at no great personal risk, to the spirit-throttling aggressions of the "totalitarians."

At the Salzburg Seminar in American Studies in 1949, our theme had been American "civilization" (the students questioned whether there was there such a thing), and our topics of discussion covered American literature, history, social thought, and the arts. Fifteen years later, in Krakow, I was still lecturing on these subjects, while increasingly convinced that my auditors in and outside the classroom were much less impressed by America's cultural achievements than by its size, variety, energy, and wealth. But it was also clear to me that, indirectly or directly, for good or ill and however described, the American influence was inescapable.

In principle, I agreed with Edmund Wilson's remark in a letter to William Faulkner that the only ideology worth subscribing to was not having any ideology. But then how was I to account for my own brand of patriotism? Why did I bridle at the sneers of America's patronizers and sing "Columbia, the Gem of the Ocean" with such vehemence? The line "Thy mandate makes tyranny tremble" did ring a little hollow when Senator McCarthy was yahooing across the United States and his stooges were sniffing for "un-American" printed material in the USIA libraries abroad. For me, however, it signified what America stood for—or ought to stand for. I associated that song with July 4 (my father's birthday) and, as Walt Whitman put it, with the vast "unconscious scenery" of "These States."

PART FIVE

I

In the early 1950s, Senator Joseph McCarthy hung over the United States like an enormous painted balloon. Watching his scowling bristly face on television had been pretty scary. The liberal press was full of stories about the lives he had wrecked, and the extent of the damage he caused has yet to be measured. There is no doubt that he brought out the worst in the worst, but he was a bugaboo of less substance than he appeared to be at the time and, in retrospect, was more of a clown. The GOP leaders who feared him and who despised his ragtag entourage without discouraging their tactics were more sinister than the jolly blackguard himself.

The smoke of McCarthyism still lingered in the late fall of 1954 when Clinton Rossiter of Cornell University, a professor of government with a strong interest in American political thought, invited me to join him and a small group in a new project. The Fund for the Republic, an adjunct of the Ford Foundation, had just commissioned him to direct a series of scholarly studies on the impact of Communism on American life. He proposed that I and four others collaborate on a volume that would deal with the subject of Communism and literature. At some point between November 1954 and May 1955, he dropped the idea of a composite volume and assigned me the job of writing my own exposition on Communism and American writers.

Philosophically conservative but politically liberal, Rossiter had been hesitant to ask either ex-Communists or inveterate rightists to join his projects. I suited him because I was a liberal with antifascist credentials who had never been a Communist Party member and because I had written a book that defined and defended an American non-Communist radical tradition. In *Men of Good Hope*, I had concentrated on eight middle-class social theorists or reformers (*progressive* was my muddy term for them), most of them Emersonians, and inspired, like me, by his humane enthusiasms. A few, notably Brooks Adams and Thorstein Veblen, were out of sync with the spirit of my hopeful company, but it was enough for me that they, too, showed a commendable distaste for plutocrats and plutocratic culture. I might have escaped a few knocks and sneers had I confined myself to their lives and personalities and muted the social commentary that exposed my own biases as well as my ignorance of political economy. But *Men of Good Hope* was the book that I wanted to write. It expressed my civic religion and got more attention than it deserved. The chapter on Brooks Adams, published earlier in an article, prompted a complimentary note from the historian Charles Beard and a postcard bearing one word, "Thanks," from Ezra Pound.

The *New York Times* announcement of the Ford project together with the names of the contributors caught the eye of J. B. Matthews, McCarthy's onetime adviser. He trashed us all but let me off with a slap. Quoting from *Men of Good Hope*, he noted with disdain my "political and ideological orientation," but his concession that I wasn't "in any sense of the word a Communist" may have blunted later suspicions or allegations that I was. Rossiter probably anticipated the potshots of right-wing legionnaires, but I think he was a little rattled by the idiosyncrasies and ineptitudes of some of his hired scholars and, in the end, by the Fund for the Republic's indifference to his series. He stubbornly pushed and cajoled the project to completion.

My resultant book, *Writers on the Left: Episodes in American Literary Communism* (1961), turned out to be a succès d'estime, the subject of a lead review in the Sunday *New York Times.* Widely cited in national periodicals and by later scholars, it was reprinted three times and pronounced a classic by a few admirers. Sales of the book were moderate, its readers likely to be writers and intellectuals and students in and outside the academy who had taken part in or followed the political debates in the 1930s or who wanted to know more about them. *Writers on the Left* had no targets, and some readers were reassured by its uncantankerous tone and by the specificity of its details. Issues that once inflamed radical vanguards were subordinated to dramatic episodes and to the personalities and literary styles of the disputants, and much of its raw material— records of ideological schisms, quotations from letters, interviews, and random esoterica—were confined to endnotes.

After its publication, I mulled over the advantages and disadvantages of writing about the living and about the safely dead. It had taken me four years to gather my information, much of it from personal interviews and after delicate negotiations. In the process, I learned a little about the ambiguities and mysteries of history. I even thought that I might be able to offer some practical illustrations of what T. S. Eliot called its "hidden corridors" and of what Tolstoy was getting at in his reflections on the battle at Borodino. A year later, I wrote an essay on the hazards of interviewing—some dos and don'ts for contemporary literary historians—with observations on the subterranean depths where unreachable truth resides. A few of these ideas were reinforced in letters to me from Lewis Mumford and Kenneth Burke. Recollection is treacherous, Mumford assured me, not only because of human fallibility but also because of the "unfathomable complexity of life." He maintained, "What we create in history or biography is myth, not representation, still less exact reproduction!" Burke didn't blame me for simplifying his views of the Communist Party but reminded me how closely his "political" ideas in the 1930s were "interwoven with personal, psychological motives" that had little to do with politics.

The Fund for the Republic's New York base was an apartment of some half-dozen rooms at 108th Street and Broadway, not far from Columbia University. Converted into an ad hoc research center, it contained the beginnings of a library of "materials of American Communism," a scattering of old periodicals, and a temperamental mimeograph. During my visits to the city, I slept on a cot in one of the rooms and stored my beer in the kitchen refrigerator. Primarily a workplace, it was also an ongoing orientation depot designed especially for someone (like me) who wasn't attuned to Marxist apologetics or to the foreign-sounding lingo of Communist Party sectarians. My colleagues had a lot to teach me, and I relied on their knowledgeable talk. But inasmuch as I had only a marginal interest in doctrinal exegesis and was preoccupied with writers and intellectuals who may have agreed with the so-called party line on certain issues but who felt no compulsion to obey it, I soon took off on my own tack. The people from the Fund for the Republic left us alone. Although I have no evidence to back me up, I daresay they expected our scholarly investigation to confirm what they already believed: that all the hysterical and politically motivated talk of Communist infiltration into the body and soul of America was largely poppycock. I agreed with this belief then and still do—which is not to deny the success of Soviet espionage in penetrating selected federal programs and agencies.

When I joined Rossiter's team in the fall of 1954, the image of the USSR as a union of democratic republics and the hope of humankind had long turned into a sick joke. To be sure, fellow travelers like me had once dismissed the "slanderous charges" against the Soviets as the machinations of the "reactionary press"—until the trumped-up treason trials in Moscow (1936–38), the Stalin-inspired "liquidation" of anarchists and Socialists during the civil war in Spain, and the U.S. Communist Party's contorted justifications of the 1939 Nazi-Soviet pact all but dissolved our unexamined loyalties. I couldn't claim to have been betrayed, since I had never believed in the Communist vision or considered myself a Marxist, much less a Stalinist. A few friends who left the Communist Party in 1939 after a fairly close association didn't appear to suffer the postwithdrawal agonies of Whittaker Chambers, who, dazzled by Communism's alluring vision, opened his eyes in time to behold its malignancies. In contrast to the simplifiers and ignoramuses he enlisted in his campaign to expose his former bosses, Chambers respected Communism as a great enemy and knew its strength. His Manichaean fable *Witness* (1952) underscores how imperfectly I had understood, much less seen, what was happening around me, how unwarranted my suppositions had been and how unreliable my guides.

To help tyros like me negotiate the Communist Party labyrinth, the Fund for the Republic paid a few "Old Bolsheviks" to serve on request as consultants. One of them, Earl Browder, leader of the American Communist Party before the opposition threw him out in 1946, gave me an interview. In his rumpled suit, he looked more like a crafty small-town businessman from Sinclair Lewis's Gopher Prairie than a leading American Communist. He had never taken the time, he told me, to visit Lenin's tomb. ("Your Protestant background?" I suggested. He laughed and agreed.) In answer to my question about writers and the Communist Party, he said that he had always been too busy to stay in touch with the arts. Writers had no place in party deliberations, for they were likely to go off half-cocked. What counted for the party was a writer's prestige, not his literary artistry.

Joseph Freeman (1897–1965)—journalist, critic, editor, poet, novelist, and, for a time, jack-of-all-trades (literary and cultural) for the Communist movement—was also on the Fund for the Republic's payroll. He became my chief counselor and opened doors to people leery of possible snoopers in the immediate aftermath of the McCarthy crusade. We got along well from the start, and until he died in 1965, he was a conscientious, if at times prickly, tutor. His letters to me, over four hundred pages of them, amounted to an informal autobiography and apologia that high-lighted the extrapolitical phases of his life. I think he wanted to show to me—and, through me, to an as-yet-undesignated pub-lic—that poetry and visions of a righteous society had always been more important to him than politics. The letters evoke a New York in the early 1920s when a happy anarchistic bohemianism prevailed. They describe his close personal and professional ties with the Greenwich Village arcadians Max Eastman and Floyd Dell; his friendships with artists in England, France, Germany, Mexico, and the Soviet Union (where he covered the Trotsky-Stalin showdown in 1927); and the events leading to his ouster from the Communist Party three years after the Comintern had detected traces of the *Bacillus trotskyensis* in his novelistic memoir *An American Testament* (1937). In these letters and in our lengthy conversations, he portrayed himself as a kind of latter-day Shelley, the poet as *Dichter*, who, "like the prophet and cenobite," com-muned in solitude with God, nature, and history, yet, "like the ancient bards and troubadours," mingled "with the people, with warriors, with leaders," with "the inner *and* outer world, with eter-nity *and* time." But because he refused to attack in print the party that had denounced and abandoned him, the U.S. Federal Bureau of Investigation hounded him and sabotaged any chance he had for a steady job. His rift with the Communist Party depressed him at the outset. In time, he came to see it as a liberation.

Notwithstanding his unstinting confidences, Joseph Freeman was at bottom a secretive person. I think he genuinely liked me, as I did him, but he was uneasy about my divagations. He wanted my book to vindicate his claim that the radicalism he espoused was of native origin, that he had repudiated Stalin's Communism because it had profaned his dream. When I first met him, he was something of an anomaly—a man on friendly terms with a few Communist Party hard-liners, with recent defectors, and with people who had long renounced that party and vigorously attacked it. Because he hadn't "named names" or "told all," the lefties in and out of the party accepted his endorsement of me as a disinterested researcher who wasn't out to get them. At the same time, some of his old companions joked about his "whoppers," considered him a bullshitter, and warned me not to swallow everything he told me. But I regarded Joe's version of events as Huckleberry Finn did Mr. Mark Twain's book about Tom Sawyer's adventures: "[H]e told the truth, mainly. There were things that he stretched, but he mainly told the truth." I learned how to adjust to Joe's alternating moods, to discount his overgenerous compliments, and to glide over his piques provoked by something I may have written or said—for example, my remark on the high percentage of Jews among the Communist intelligentsia. My lukewarm response to his verse probably disappointed him, but I gave him no reason to doubt my respect and affection. He was a charmer with a big bag of diverting stories about himself and others, an ingratiating teacher, an enthusiast and cynic, and a scarred veteran of the culture wars.

One needed a tough hide to survive these wars. By temperament, Joe was less suited to the political hurly-burly than, say, his bête noire Sidney Hook, who had so well described their New York City milieu: a battlefront where young Jewish intellectuals with knives in their brains rudely clashed with their classmates and teachers. Freeman excelled in debate (he captained Columbia's debating team), aided no doubt by his oratorical and argumentative skills and his feel for his audiences. But he preferred the lyre to the hatchet. I think he saw himself as one attuned to secret and sacred things and alert to emblems and omens. His long letters, blending quotidian detail with poetic expostulation, reported startling coincidences and remarkable encounters—one with the aforementioned Whittaker Chambers, former member of the Columbia wrestling team and moody poet, whom Freeman brought to the *New Masses*.

Freeman's version of his first encounter with Chambers is an episode Dostoyevskian in flavor that Alger Hiss's attorney asked Freeman (without success) to repeat in a courtroom hearing. The year was 1928, and Joe Freeman was editing the *New Masses*. His brother asked him to do something for Whittaker Chambers, a poet unhappily stuck in the Communist Party daily and eager to work on a literary paper. "Bring him around," said Joe. So Joe, Chambers, and a few others met at a German restaurant on Third Avenue and East Sixteenth Street, where there was much eating and drinking. Chambers suggested that he and Joe swear *Bruderschaft*, by which he meant cutting wrists and mingling blood. The "short, stocky, blue-eyed" Chambers grasped Joe's arm "in an iron grip" and was about to saw away when the bartender batted the knife out of Chambers's hand, after which there were apologies. By then it was much too late for Chambers to get back to Long Island. Joe invited him to spend the night in Brooklyn, where Joe was living with his brother and sister-in-law. On the way, a partially sobered Chambers improvised "magnificent" Whitmanesque verses. Right there and then, Joe decided to put him on the staff of the *New Masses*. In the Brooklyn kitchen where Joe's sister-in-law was about to prepare bacon and eggs and coffee for the sodden poets, Chambers fell on his knees, kissed the hem of her kimono, and wailed "in a strange low voice, 'Forgive me! Forgive me!'" as tears streamed down "his pale plump cheeks." He left the next morning, bidding a polite good-bye.

Between 1928 and 1932, Chambers justified Joe's expectations by writing some "powerful verse" and a story called "Listen to Their Voices," first published in the Communist Party press and then dramatized for left-wing acting groups all over the country. Joe exited from the paper to write a book. When he returned in 1932, Chambers had vanished—"in a fit of bohemianism." Sometime later, a bearded Chambers was spotted on Eighth Street posing as "a secret agent for the Russians." This was nonsense, Joe concluded, because a secret agent wouldn't tell you he was one and because the Russians wouldn't use a neurotic poet to spy for them.

By 1942, Joe was out of the party and out of politics. A *Life* magazine editor commissioned him to write a five-thousand-word essay on twenty-five years of Russian revolution. In two months, he turned out a thirty-thousand-word piece. Mr. Henry Luce liked it so much that he sent printed copies to the White House and to every senator, House member, state governor, top military and business leader, university president, and so on. Joseph Davies, ambassador to Moscow, invited Joe to become his "special assistant." For unexplained reasons, Joe turned down the offer, but he was decidedly interested in the possibility of working full-time for Luce. He was told that he first had to be screened by *Life's* foreign editor, Whittaker Chambers.

Freeman reports of this encounter: "The poet I had taken on the *NM* in 1928 was now very fat, very heavy; his bullet head stuck out through a crew haircut; his eyes were hard; a number of his teeth were missing. I had not seen him in years—but recognized him at once. He was sitting behind a large desk like a big executive in a Grade-B movie: he *was* a big executive." Chambers showed no sign of recognizing Freeman and questioned him about his political views and property, to which Freeman responded that he had none of either. Chambers exclaimed, "No man can serve his country loyally unless he is invested in its soil," which Freeman found an odd comment coming "from the rip-roaring literary Bolshevik I had known in the early thirties." When Chambers, a Quaker, asked if Joe believed in God, the latter replied, "In my own way." The interview was over, and Joe was dismissed without even a good-bye.

Presidential reputations are mutable. There is no doubt that Richard Milhous Nixon's will fluctuate and that the statesman will, for some historians, efface the clown and villain. While he flourished, it was hard for liberal academicians with little knowledge of the inner workings of American politics to judge him adequately. I once saw him fleetingly in Northampton, where his daughter (the dark intense one who married the grandson of President Eisenhower) was then a student at Smith College. President Nixon was getting out of a car warily, I recall, as one might step on a minefield. Nixon in the flesh was less real to me than the Nixon of my animus—a bogeyman who had descended in a cloud of McCarthyism. Like many of his adversaries, I simplified him and underestimated his abilities, if not his character. I thought then, as I do now, that he was both synthetic and ignoble.

Since his death, RMN has grown steadily less endearing, but he has become more interestingly complicated than your usual run of conservative Republicans. He was exposed to the public glare from his first cut-and-thrust political campaign until he resigned his office, yet he remained all the while something of a puzzlement. Neither scholars nor fiction writers have quite situated him in presidential history. John Updike remembers "hooting at the Checkers speech as an undergraduate" yet feeling at the same time "something touching about him, something well-meaning and inept." I can understand what Updike means, but I could make no such extenuation in the 1960s, when Nixon struck me as a pustule of political contagion and a kind of imposter.

FDR had been the radio president. His voice could smile and frown, jeer and reassure, take you into his consciousness. My Nixon (to distinguish him from the RMN of the history books and biographies) was a creature of television—like Ronald Reagan, but he never managed it with Reaganesque ease. The more earnestly he spoke—as, for example, on those critical occasions when he was reassuring a national audience he was indeed "as clean as a hound's tooth," when he unctuously described his wife's modest furless coat, or when he vehemently protested that he intended to keep the gift of the little dog his family loved—the phonier he sounded. These public confessions didn't sit well with the cynical and sophisticated (a problem that was of small consequence really), but they saved his political neck.

Nixon had more than a touch of Malvolio, and there is a certain pathos in his pomposity and physical awkwardness, in the gap between his real and fancied selves, in his unmusical profanity. He was at his worst when acting presidential or talking sports like a regular Joe and being aggressively friendly. What kept him, one wonders, from being simple? Why were his sentences so thick and heavy, his smiles so mirthless? Who were his real friends? What did they like about him? Did he ever say any-thing more resonantly quotable than "I am not a crook"? Why does he figure in novels, plays, and satires more than any other president in his waning century? "People are more likely to be frightened or angered into taking sensible or honorable positions than reasoned or shamed into supporting them," reads an entry from my journal (January 24, 1973), which continues, "I some-times think that Nixon's unpopularity at the moment has less to do with his impeachable acts, his arrogance, and the overexten-sion of his presidential prerogatives than it has to do with his alleged diddling of his income tax returns."

The unloyal opposition I belonged to had nothing to do with RMN's untragical fall. Watergate sank him, which is another way of saying that he unintendingly collaborated with his ene-mies and assisted in his own prosecution. Our detestation of him was almost as much aesthetic as political. We were embarrassed by his appearance, style, manners, posturings, and fakery; by his macho voice talking football; by his trying to be what he wasn't. Nothing about Watergate was grand or tragic; no mighty hero crashed. The president's attempt to explain it as the impulsive act of a few overzealous henchmen provoked vindictive glee. How emblematically right that the "leader of the free world," when addressing the nation in the scandal's aftermath, should stumble over the word integrity.

After Nixon's tearful decampment, President Gerald Rudolph Ford's succession seemed anticlimactic, and the new president himself was someone neither to cheer nor to groan about. His pardoning of RMN wasn't unexpected (I took it to be an act of party loyalty, not a "corrupt bargain"), although it irritated thou-sands of Nixon's ill-wishers who had wanted to see Nixon nailed to the wall. More pertinent was whether the new president was up to his office. President Johnson's jibe that Gerry Ford had scrambled his brains playing football without a helmet was widely quoted, if not his ruder quip that Ford couldn't fart and chew gum at the same time. Bruce Bliven, a resident of Stanford University's Kingscote Garden during my stay there and onetime editor of the *New Republic*, likened Gerald Ford to Herbert

Hoover without the high collar. Bliven wrote in his Christmas message: "[Ford] does one good thing and nine bad, making him one of the notorious Washington ten percenters. Who would have thought we would have three presidents in a row who make McKinley look good?"

I took for granted what seemed to be the consensus that President Ford wasn't overtly smart (an opinion disputed by my brother, a law professor, who had been much impressed by Ford's lecture to one of his classes), but in any event, it didn't seem to matter. I attributed my apathy in part to the political exhaustion that set in after RMN was helicoptered out of Washington in August 1974. Besides, Ford was only a temporarily licensed caretaker of the presidency. I took a mean-spirited pleasure in his campaign gaffes and hardly noticed his emerging difference from the Republican hatchet men.

Were I writing President Ford's obituary, it might read something like this: "He would have looked better had he lived in quieter times and been less of a GOP yes-man and hadn't saddled himself to his failed, yet ever-scheming, predecessor. Gerald Ford displayed no signs of greatness, but he was able to unruffle the ruffled and to inspire trust, not in a calculating way, but simply by being friendly and decent. Unguileful (like Melville's trusting sea captain in the novella *Benito Cereno*) and hesitant about rocking political boats, he is said to have said that he enjoyed his short span in office. He wanted America to live up to its ideals, and he believed in good things—his wife and golf." 🍂

III

Embarked on the Rossiter project, I shuttled between Northampton and New York reading out-of-print books and rummaging through files of short-lived periodicals. A few of them disintegrated as I held them in my hands. I searched for letters and manuscripts of old radicals and wrote to and tried to interview writers and artists who had come of age before I was born. One of them, Max Eastman (1883–1969), became a pivotal figure in my research.

I decided early that a nobody who wanted to be taken seriously by somebody like Max Eastman, not a notably modest man, had better show that he had dug a bit into his life and work. In January 1957, when I first approached him, I had read most of his books and knew quite a lot about his transformation from friend to foe of the Soviet experiment and about his views on socialism as well. My long letter made no reference to his current opinions and confined itself to the period before the crimes of the Stalin regime had pushed him toward the radical Right. It was addressed to the "romantic rebel," former editor of *The Masses*, who in the course of an adventurous life had encountered Mark Twain, Anatole France, Sigmund Freud, and Eugene Debs. He had known Isadora Duncan, Charlie Chaplin, Leon Trotsky, Randolph Bourne, and George Santayana and ineffectually brawled with Ernest Hemingway. Quite a lot of sex figured in his revolutionary acrobatics. I was hesitant, I said in my letter, to lump him and all of his rebel contemporaries into a single throng of joyous amateurs: "You agreed on your antipathies but differed in your aesthetic standards and in your political goals."

Eastman graciously replied. He had read my letter, he said, with "an approving interest" and thought I was going about my task in the right way. Still, he emphasized, I must keep in mind that neither he nor Floyd Dell, his coeditor on *The Masses*, thought the "revolutionary" poems sent to them were any good. He asserted that politics never moved him to write poetry and that he would have liked to "abolish politics altogether." He recalled hearing Randolph Bourne play "my favorite melody from Brahms, his hunched and crippled figure perched on a big book on a piano stool." Other letters followed, and from time to time we'd have the daylong talks he professed to enjoy. All in all, I found him genial and generous and touchingly vain. There was something godlike in his looks and manner as he parted the tall grass on his sequestered beach in Chilmark on Martha's Vineyard and walked naked into the ocean. His guests, young and old, were expected to follow suit, as I did.

Eastman was still seeing something of his old companion Floyd Dell when I began *Writers on the Left*. At Freeman's suggestion, I had written to Dell, who replied at length in good-humored letters about the joys and tribulations of the radical movements in Wilsonian America. Ostensibly, he and Freeman were again fast friends after a frosty interlude. It turned out, however, that Dell had long resented what he thought were serious omissions and misstatements about him in Freeman's self-exculpating *An American Testament*. Given my touchy relations with Freeman at this moment, I was loath to antagonize him further. Dell warned me against swallowing what were to him Freeman's self-serving inaccuracies, but he was pleased that I hadn't taken for real the Communist literati's caricature of him as a sex-obsessed hedonist.

Meeting Dell and Eastman and some of their younger contemporaries filled out my picture of a bohemian scene I was first introduced to in the books of James Gibbons Huneker and in the writings of assorted utopians, anarchists, and social prophets. I by no means subscribed to their directives for salvation, but I believed that in their best moments, they exhibited an admirable social ethic. This was illustrated to me one night in Max Eastman's West Thirteenth Street flat as I watched E. E. Cummings change from his charmingly witty self into an unfunny assailant of blacks and Jews. Eastman ordered his friend and fellow conservative to shut up or get out. He would not listen to such talk in his own house. So Cummings left and dispelled an illusion.

Edmund Wilson was, in his own way, no less rectitudinous. I had begun to read him at length in my late teens, and he became for me a trustworthy interpreter of the literary scene. Like many of my generation, I relied on his clear and vigorous exposition of difficult modern authors, which he managed to do without vulgarizing them or resorting to fashionable jargon. I met him in

1943 and continued to see him off and on until his death in 1972. Arrogant and irascible at times and more than glad to deliver judgments, he was a patient listener and interrogator with a stock of stories about himself and his literary friends. Over the years, I heard his off-the-cuff table talk, for example, the plot of a ghost story he never got around to write; his thoughts on Hemingway's suicide (it made him feel lonely and a bit afraid); his habit of signing the name "Robert Watson" on hotel registers during his tom-catting days; two responses to his novel, *I Thought of Daisy,* one from a suicidal Englishman, to whom it brought relief, the other from a Spanish woman who wrote that her husband had died of a heart attack while reading it ("So you see," he told me, "I can save or kill"); how his fancy about winning the Nobel Prize crashed with a thud after an official-looking document from Sweden turned out to be a crank letter alerting him to a world conspiracy of assassins who could change their sexes and communicate tele-pathically.

Neither Wilson nor Eastman warmed to the subject of my book on the American literary left, even though the former pro-nounced it both "intelligent and accurate" and the latter assured me that it would become a standard work. Eastman could neither forgive nor forget the atrocious diatribes against him by some of the former Communists I was seeking to interview. Wilson was indifferent to the jibes of his critics, but the political and literary debates that once engaged him now seemed "stale and distaste-ful." Both agreed that I hadn't paid enough attention to East-man's later writings or gone to the mat over the issue of Marxism and its fallacies. I had given too much space to the ins and outs of moldy controversies and scanted, as Wilson put it, "the more solid and important works that some of us eventually wrote." That was so, but then, as I told myself, *Writers* wasn't written as an exercise in Marxist apologetics, and I wasn't the person to write such a work. Nor was I upset by the charge that I had relived, rather than reexamined or thought through, a period of ideological grappling and Talmudic hairsplitting. I did suggest, however, that a historian can become so steeped and soaked in a historical event or period that, for a time, he loses his own identity. Thus, if I had an expository method, it was the trick of entering into the minds of my subjects and speaking in their own idioms. This enabled me to set down without comment their insights and fatuities.

Edmund Wilson had reluctantly addressed some of the questions I put to him about his brief Marxist phase and was readier to lecture me on "neglected" American authors than to resurrect musty sectarian polemics. Having discovered Poe, Emerson, and Thoreau in his youth, he had gone on reading American authors most of his peers had never heard of (much less read) and, like his friend Van Wyck Brooks, disrespecting Americanists who presumed to teach a literature they had only skimmed. Wilson never softened his critique of jingoists and plutocrats, but he internalized American democratic culture. He wanted his readers to know it and be proud of it. While working on his chronicle of Civil War writing, it irked him that so many of the books he felt obliged to examine were out of print or hard to obtain. His frustrations may partly explain why he got caught up in a long-incubating project to publish the best American authors, no matter how obscure, in a uniform set of modestly priced volumes. Literary friends and a few publishers backed him up, but bad luck and his own imperious temperament frustrated his plan. A decade after his death in 1972, it was realized or at least approximated in the Library of America.

IV

From the 1950s on, Edmund Wilson lived mostly in Wellfleet, Massachusetts, on lower Cape Cod, where a trickle and then a stream of artists, writers, academics, and assorted intellectuals had begun to rent space in the summer months. They formed a less cohesive community than did their predecessors in Provincetown twenty-five years earlier, but it didn't take long before they began to act like old settlers and to watch their own lives turn into legend. In 1941, Wilson, who, like his friend Dos Passos, had links with both the earlier group and the newcomers, bought a capacious all-season Wellfleet house a few years after he had married Mary McCarthy, the third of his four wives and an electric presence in Trotskyist literary circles.

I had met Mary McCarthy at Smith College in 1943, when her famous husband was inexpertly and unhappily delivering a set of lectures. Handsome and vivacious, she was already fabled for her daggerish wit, and her visits to Northampton furnished occasions for dinners and parties. No obvious signs of a contentious rupture in her marriage were then in evidence. Not long after her divorce, she returned to summertime Wellfleet with a new husband seven years her junior and charmed and dominated the guests invited to her cottage on Pamet Point. There, in her role of aproned matron, she served nutritious soups and vitamin-intact vegetables. At evening beach parties, you could find her with other skinny-dippers vigorously toweling herself before blazing driftwood fires. Then and later, she was natural and friendly and given to kind gestures. I liked her for, among other reasons, her unfashionable approval of William Dean Howells, a writer whose irony and realism she savored.

Dwight Macdonald, an ally in many of Mary's political and marital altercations, had been coming to Cape Cod since 1944. We were neighbors on Slough Pond, one of Thoreau's sacred fonts and an idyllic place where wearing clothes wasn't insisted upon and every swim was a baptism. Although physically awkward and not much of an athlete, Macdonald was chief organizer of our periodic softball games, which he hugely enjoyed and in which he displayed the same derisiveness, rudeness, and good humor he brought to political and intellectual contests. Macdonald was impulsive and romantic (he would have denied the latter) and drawn to underdogs (Trotsky against Stalin, the Spanish republicans against Franco, Mary McCarthy against Edmund Wilson) and to the persecuted and humiliated everywhere. He was most splendidly himself in his magazine *Politics,* which I religiously read from its first issue to its last (1944–49), beguiled by its anarchistic music, its humanity, and its assaults against J. Edgar Hoover, Henry Luce, the Soviet Politburo, Henry Wallace, Lyndon Johnson. He dared to sound ridiculous and scorned "mitigating circumstances"—for him, good was good, and bad was bad. Friendly, tactless, and argumentative, he was often "assful," in Mark Twain's sense of the word, and appallingly honest.

In memorabilia about the Wellfleet and Truro circle of writers and artists, Dwight Macdonald has sometimes mistakenly been depicted as a kind of master of revels. I think he was too caught up in his magazines and causes to socialize outside his cultural and political ken. The novelist Edwin O'Connor may be a more fitting candidate for that title. He had lived longer in Wellfleet than all but a few of the literary residents, and his friends included not only the public names, the makers and subjects of news, but also town oddballs and diverse frequenters of Newcomb Hollow Beach along with their wives, children, and dogs. A graduate of Notre Dame University, his religious faith deep and private, O'Connor was typed as a comedian. Indeed, he was a droll man, a friend of Fred Allen and Abe Burrough, and a talented raconteur whose accents—Irish, German, Jewish, Yankee—sounded wonderfully authentic. At bottom, he was reserved, sad, and sardonic—but not judgmental toward the alcoholics and misfits and shaky men and women who cluttered the Wellfleet summer scene and whom he contemplated with a priestly eye. His targets tended to be pompous people, boosters, bluffers, vulgarians, zealots. Dickens was his favorite author. *The Last Hurrah* (1956), a novel modeled on the career of Boston political boss James Michael Curley, made him famous and also rich enough to build a house and studio in our neck of the woods. There, he served good food and drink and entertained us with his observations on President Kennedy's "summer White House" in Hyannisport, where he was a frequent and favored guest. In the end, Curley became an incubus, especially after Hollywood turned *The Last Hurrah* into a parody and Curley decided to cash in on the renown of his fictive self.

Ed O'Connor had links with the New York entertainment industry, especially radio and theater; I don't think he knew or cared very much about that corner of Manhattan to which I had begun to commute in the 1950s. In the past half century, several generations of nonconformist intellectuals and artists had made New York City their mecca. The crop that came of age in the 1930s was no easier for me to categorize than their nineteenth- and early twentieth-century equivalents. Nonetheless, although I was older than most of them, they made me feel younger—and certainly more provincial. They had outgrown their childhoods faster than I had mine. They seemed to be smart and contentious and ambitious, held in equilibrium by their shared antipathies and by a social and aesthetic consensus. A large number of them were Jewish (as, of course, I was) but linked by a common culture I didn't share. The term "New York Intellectuals," however, makes them sound more cohesive than they were. In the *Partisan Review*, taken over from its Stalinist founders in 1936, they had a magazine small in circulation but large in influence. Historian Richard Hofstadter referred to it as the "house organ" of the anti-Stalinist literary left, but one has only to sample the output of its editors and contributors—among them Philip Rahv, William Phillips, Dwight Macdonald, George Orwell, Delmore Schwartz, Isaac Rosenfeld, Sidney Hook, Edmund Wilson, Daniel Bell, Nathan Glazer, and Meyer Schapiro—to appreciate their bristling disparities. As a group, they had not yet acquired their distinctive patina when I first encountered them, and my own contacts with this energetic and ambitious elite were still marginal. I had never felt easy in their New York. My New York was largely musical and theatrical, less Whitman's "Manahatta" or Scott Fitzgerald's magical city than an uncharted metropolis to camp in and goggle at and a haunt of authors—a fusion of bars, jazz spots, theaters, subway trains. Their New York was home turf, and they were the aborigines. They knew the trails and clearings of the five boroughs, camped in Greenwich Village savannas, powwowed in restaurants and bookshops.

Tough debaters and fast-talkers, confident and competitive and often rude, they could make you feel thick-witted and wither you with a look. They had sharpened their polemical skills in the alcoves of their respective academies and were veterans of ideological wars while still in their teens. Even those who liked me well enough (or so I fancied) sized me up as a soft, cautious, and unconfrontational provincial. I, in turn, bolstered my self-regard with the thought that I probably knew better than they "the varied and ample land" that lay west of the Hudson and much more about the United States in general. Clearly I was an outsider, but then my designated role in Rossiter's project on the impact of Communism was that of detached historian. I knew nothing and cared less about the vendettas, past or present, of competing Marxist sects, and I trusted such benevolent ironists as Kenneth Burke to straighten out what he described in a letter to me as the "tangle within the tangle."

Burke's books and articles stirred up many persons of my generation and perspective, subverting alike hagiography and adolescent iconoclasm. He drew ingenious analogies in the spirit and trenchant style of Thorstein Veblen. I met him in the pastoral setting of Bennington College, where I was moonlighting a few days a week in 1950–51. I don't know what the students made of his pronouncements, which were not easily grasped, but to his younger colleagues, he was the ultimate critic, Aristotle with a dash of Mr. Magoo. His "good works," as one of his devotees put it, were "C" words: "curiosity, cooperation, connection." I poured over his witty footnotes and asides and incorporated his apothegms into my own reading of American literature and history.

But it was the historian Richard Hofstadter who eased me into the company of the as-yet-uncanonized circle of "New York Intellectuals." He was an outsider, too, not because he hailed from another city and was only half Jewish (in fact, the *Partisan Review* circle respected his books and enjoyed his company), but because, unlike most of his friends, he was a professional scholar with no hankering for the literary life or for a career outside academia. Having passed through a radically leftist phase, he adhered to what he described to me as his "liberal-conservative-elitist-ethical brand of private socialism," and although he approved of my trying to get "the ethical-utopian element back to the center of things," he was more wary than I of the antinomian impulses in both past and present America. I was then deep into Emerson, whom I pronounced to be "our Atlantic and Pacific, our national Proteus, our ever-replenishing dinner," and the last of our clerisy who mediated between the spirit and the marketplace. I still adhered to Randolph Bourne's injunction to the pragmatists that "vision must constantly outshoot technique."

Richard Hofstadter disdained the New Left's radical enthusiasts in the 1960s, but unlike some anti-Communist liberals, he had nothing good to say for right-wing true believers in the Congress and State Department. He was rather taken with the distinction A. M. Schlesinger Jr. drew in *The Vital Center* between the liberal and Marxian concepts of the class struggle. Hofstadter paraphrased Schlesinger, "You must have class struggle since the only alternative is class domination; the problem is to keep it in bounds so that it doesn't destroy the common fabric of principle that holds society together." As he aged, Hofstadter grew philosophically (and ruefully) more conservative. ("I never thought I would come to this," he wrote me in 1963, "but I suspect that by the time I'm an old man, I will be locked in the arms of Metternich.") One could sense as much in his alertness to symptoms of disaster and in a latent melancholy that his elaborate joke telling and bursts of high spirits never quite extinguished. We were friends and collaborators for twenty-four years. I saw him a week before he died of leukemia in 1970. Propped in a chair beside his bed and fearfully emaciated, he spoke as if he had dismissed any thought of mortality, but though outwardly composed, he had the look of a deserted man who was already seeing what we couldn't see. Twenty years afterward, Alfred Kazin wrote me of Hofstadter's ineradicable presence: "Peter Gay said last May that he missed Dick every month . . . And I said, every hour. How he sticks to us. Or as I like to say to myself in my busy journal of my life here on earth, 'the dead refuse to leave you.' And we refuse to leave them. So there's some hope to this daily marriage of heaven and hell."

Kazin sticks, too. A brave and honorable man, his intense self-centeredness was subsumed by a natural nobility. I saw him continuously during the two years he spent in the Connecticut Valley (1953–55), first at Smith College, where he would have liked to stay, and then at nearby Amherst, a community that at that time did not take kindly to unconstrained talkers from New York City. He might as well have sported a turban and worn brass earrings. In the summer of 1953, we put together an anthology of Emerson's writings, reading aloud to each other and selecting what we considered to be his incandescent moments and ephemeral flash points. It was great fun and a work of love, yet *Emerson: A Modern Anthology* sank without a ripple (Kazin explained: "Those who don't know RWE don't know how good the book is. Those who do probably feel no need to read it.")

In his letters to me, Kazin often reflected on his status between "professional Jews," for whom a "mild anxiety about Israel amounted to treason," and the critics who faulted him for focusing so intently on his Jewishness. His failure to obtain a tenured professorship at a major eastern institution—blackballed, he believed, by an Ivy League elite—at first embittered him. How could the literary dons of Amherst and Yale conduct their mandarin exercises in critical reading in the teeth of student illiteracy? It would have been easy for him, he told me, to parlay his "wit and wisdom into a 'power' position." This was no vain boast, but his longing to put his "thought and life fully on paper" proved stronger than his wish for academic acclaim.

We remained "brothers" but distantly close, guardedly intimate. At moments, he made me feel an Esau to his Jacob—I even mispronounced the word *pogrom*. Notwithstanding, he cherished me as a reliable sounding board and gratefully noted my criticisms. About my own work, he had little to say beyond a few gracious commendations or an insertion here and there on points of disagreement. He simply had too much to read and write and do to divert himself from matters that to him were of pressing importance. I dare say he would have opened up had I pushed him, but he wasn't an attentive listener. He was a friend, if not exactly a confidant, and he was a powerful egoist whose self-absorption was only less than his moral courage.

For a long time, Kazin spoke of himself as a "writer" and made fun of "professors," but like many freelance writers after World War II, he needed the academy to survive. Perforce he became an itinerant evangelist of letters. Not until the later years of what he termed his "maelstrom century" did he occupy a permanent pulpit. By then, he was a public figure fixed in the annals of American letters: essayist, autobiographer, social critic, cultural historian. He stood for something else as well, the latter-day prophet, often embarrassingly outspoken, who rebuked careerists out for money and power and who swore by Emerson, Thoreau, Melville, Whitman, Emily Dickinson. No more than Walt Whitman, the Gnostic rabbi of Manhattan, was he accepted wholly and comfortably by the Ivy League WASPs. Invited to lecture or to spend a semester or two as their visitor, he wasn't asked to stay. In the end, he settled and flourished on his own native grounds.

So did Irving Howe, who, in the taxonomy of literary historians, belongs, like Kazin, to the genus *intelligentsia New Yorkensis*, even though neither perfectly fits the ascription. Both started out as socialists without necessarily subscribing to the programs of the variegated socialist factions. Both, at least as I perceived them, were New York City fauna, and both had sardonic things to say about ex-leftists turned new conservatives. But Howe had always seemed to me testier and more combative than Kazin (himself no slouch in political exchange), harsher in his put-downs, and much less given to public self-exploration. He fiercely believed and disbelieved, yet he also gladly learned, and he liked to try out new ideas and to clarify old ones. When he reviewed my Ford Foundation volume on American literary Communism, he swatted me for being almost criminally lenient ("liberal") in my treatment of the "card-carrying" and fellow-traveling writers on the left, but his curiosity characteristically vitiated his biases. In subsequent letters, he raised new issues. At what point, he queried, did American intellectuals start calling themselves "liberal"? Probably not until the later nineteenth century, he thought: Emerson was neither a liberal nor an antiliberal; Thoreau exhibited antiliberal strains. Howells was Howe's candidate for the first "liberal" American novelist. Howe asked me what links, if any, I found between homegrown radical sectarians of the past and the early intrepid moral protesters he met in the early 1960s. He argued that their response to Vietnam wasn't "political," as his was; rather, it expressed a kind of rectitude or "pure" protest that was "total" without being "totalitarian." Had I ever met a Communist, he asked "who talked Bolshevik but thought Emerson?" He wondered whether a popularized Emersonianism had pervaded all of American culture by the end of the century, even the socialism of Eugene Debs. Howe detected the virus in himself.

Early in 1963, Howe stopped in for some advice. Stanford University was considering him for a professorship in American studies. He needed coaching (which I provided) on how to present himself and what to say about his approach to that hazy interdepartmental discipline. This was the decade when the east-to-west academic exodus was in full flood. Palo Alto and Berkeley had become gilded Botany Bays for middle-aged East Coast professors in flight from sagging marriages undermined by their irregular romances with students: the West Coast represented a paradigm shift, new love in a new clime. Here was the stuff for a spate of tragic-comic college novels with an archetypal plot: a professor falls in love with a young woman prettier, smarter, and more exciting than his shopworn wife, who has drudged for him, raised their brood in mean surroundings, and grown obsolescent in the process; the professor feels he has earned his eminence and can no longer deny himself what Providence has decreed, so he dumps the wife with varying degrees of anguish and remorse. Howe got the Stanford job but didn't adjust easily to his students or colleagues nor they to him, and he returned to his familiar Manhattan canyons.

V

I completed my study of the leftist writers at the Center for Advanced Study in the Behavioral Sciences in Palo Alto, California. A creation of the Ford Foundation and already four years old when I got there in 1968, the center still prompted witticisms about the "leisure of the theory class." The "behavioral sciences" normally comprised disciplines beyond my ken—sociology, psychology, economics, linguistics, anthropology—and the term had a jargonish ring to me. At the center, philosophy, history, and legal studies were incorporated into the rubric, and even students of literature managed to slip under the behavioral tent of this Stanford "Think Tank." That was the center's facetious designation, suggested, perhaps, by what one reporter called its "glass-walled study rooms . . . hidden away in an oak-studded hilltop" overlooking "beautiful gardens, the Stanford University campus, and San Francisco Bay." In time, less disinterested laboratories were funded to educate the misinformed on social and political issues, but the center's chief function was to provide a setting for unhampered intellectual exchange. (So far as I recall, no one thought it worth mentioning that of the forty-seven research fellows in our session, only two were women.)

The Center for Advanced Study in the Behavioral Sciences was heralded as a sequestered retreat where scholars and theorists could recharge their batteries and break out of tired routines, and so it turned out to be—at least for the first three weeks. Thereafter, the contemplative atmosphere slowly dissipated, and the hesitant tappings of typewriters could be heard as pure speculation gave way to the production of books and articles, the hard evidence of thought. A fair amount of gingerly interdisciplinary discourse went on in the ad hoc workshops, but a few of us never cottoned to the concepts or the language of the behavioral scientists. Our most profitable exchanges, usually unplanned and extrabehavioral, took place at lunchtime, at coffee breaks, and during casual walks when new acquaintances showed themselves in unexpected light. One afternoon on a Palo Alto hillside, I looked for birds and discussed the origin of words with the logician W. V. Quine and straightway became a devotee of his vade mecum, Skeat's *Etymological Dictionary*. Once, at the end of the day, after most of the fellows had left the center, the linguist and literary theorist Roman Jakobson brought out a bowl of caviar and a bottle of chilled vodka and chanted Mayakovski from the tabletop.

Kingscote Gardens, where I lived, was a comfortable nondescript apartment hotel on the Stanford campus. The Berkeley professor, critic, and novelist Mark Schorer lived there between weekends. He was about to finish his immense and smoldering biography of Sinclair Lewis, most of which he wrote during our year at the center. By the time it had "swelled and groaned" (his words) into completion, he had started to turn against his hero, whose latter-day assfulness, ludicrous antics, and manic excesses pained him to the extreme. I was reminded of Mark's story, published earlier, about a slum kid's attachment to a mongrel dog. When the dog is killed by a car, the boy's response isn't tears but fury, and the story ends with the boy beating the dead dog with a stick. I think that was what Schorer was doing to the Lewis he had originally admired. When I interviewed Lewis in 1948 for the *Reporter*, he was already a wrecked man, a casualty of booze, with an emaciated and ravaged face. Yet, as I reported then, "something gay and youthful looked through the death's-head," and so it does in Mark Schorer's funny, dense, and uncompromising book.

Bruce Bliven, a former editor of the *New Republic* and a useful informant much disliked by Edmund Wilson, was a permanent resident on the Stanford campus. So was Alexander Kerensky, who had briefly headed the Russian state until the Bolsheviks threw him out. Every morning, I exchanged bows with Mr. Kerensky, a thin erect man with close-cropped gray hair, as he took off for the nearby Hoover Library and I for my tranquil office in the Center for Advanced Study in the Behavioral Sciences. I chose it for its absence of a view, but in the morning one could hear the quail whistling and see a chunk of the bay. Besides the birds and flowering hills, little was going on in either Stanford or Palo Alto to tempt me from my desk: not the student scene (flocks of white convertibles) or the art museum (with its iron conversation piece of Mr. and Mrs. Stanford and their seraphic son and the antique locomotive in the basement); not the short-sleeved tourists and tanned retirees feeding in the local cafeterias, the endless flow of cars on the freeways, the cloned cities strung along the highway from Palo Alto to San Francisco, or—after an initial look—the enormous interchangeable supermarkets.

The wonders of the West Coast gradually lost their novelty for me after weekend jaunts to Berkeley and trips to San Francisco to meet old Communist Mike Gold. Gold was suspicious, he had written me, of careerist scholars "cannibalizing the history of Communism and Socialism and all social thought in this country, not engaged themselves, observers and critics only, as though they were spies or something." Still, Joe Freeman had vouched for me, so Gold invited me to "come to dinner some night." Gold lived in the Haight-Ashbury area with his French-born wife and their two factory-worker sons. The rooms in the spacious tenement they occupied were airy and sprawlable, but after I arrived clutching two jugs of wine, we did most of our talking in the kitchen. Any stiffness between us quickly disappeared. He accepted me for what I was, not of his persuasion but not a spy either and trustworthy enough to join the crowd he had invited to celebrate Bastille Day. Mike presided. He acknowledged the setbacks the Communist movement had suffered since the Khrushchev revelations two years before but admonished us to keep the faith—after all, there was China. I thought of the Christians gathered in the Roman catacombs as Roman centurions tramped overhead.

Gold kept searching for signs that presaged the revival of a "creative and hopeful socialism," and at sixty-seven, his confidence was firm. After more than forty years in the movement, he still believed "as fully as . . . when a kid that working for capitalism is a waste of one's life on earth and working for socialism is health, goodness, and glory enough to fill a lifetime," but he had abandoned what he called his "vituperations." Reliving his past, he was often surprised by his own brilliance yet chagrined by his disputatious youthful self, the vehement polemicist careless of facts, who flourished at a time when everyone was a "leftist." He was cheered by the resurgence of radical youth in the late 1950s and by its commitment to "the great issue of world peace and human freedom." He prophesied (at the same time apologizing for "soapboxing") that the 1930s writers would rise from the grave "where the Ivy League Kafkas thought they had buried them." He'd lost much of his buoyant confidence, but he wasn't ruefully self-analytic like some ex-Reds and would have rebuffed me had I even intimated that the Communist Party had hobbled his mind and misdirected his marked literary gifts or made him insensitive to the less obvious omens of impending social disorder. For some reason, I didn't mention to him an incident I reported in my journal for November 1958.

Aboard early morning bus en route to Palo Alto after staying up most of the night at 448 Waller Street in San Francisco, drinking wine with Mike Gold. Woke up just in time to get off at what seemed to be the Palo Alto Supermarket stop. Everything looked familiar and yet different in the blinding sunlight. Took me some time to realize that this was another supermarket in another city. Accosted in my dazed state by a fattish young man wearing khaki trousers and a clean white shirt. Would I talk to him, he asks. I look to him like someone who knows where he is and where he's going. As for himself, he's chronically at sea, in love with his sister. Of course, he assured me, he didn't want to go to bed with her, but he's been sufficiently perturbed to quit law school and take a job in the post office. In fact, he was on his way to visit her when he spotted me, the confident carefree fellow with a knapsack. I had no advice to give him, nor did he ask for any. We chatted peacefully on the curbstone where I waited for the next bus. "God bless," he called, as it stopped to pick me up.

VI

My search for living relics of the Socialist movement took me to Monrovia, California, to see the reformer and publicist Upton Sinclair. Joe Freeman had advised me not to miss the opportunity:

He is now 80 and still full of beans. He is also the only man of any age I have ever known who feels he has lived the perfect life. He told the newsmen who interviewed him on his birthday that he would not take back one single deed he has ever done or a single one of the millions of words he had ever written because, while he was not always right, he always tried to do the right thing, and this, it seems, is an absolute guarantee for avoiding all error in thought, speech, and action for leading a blameless life.

Sinclair and Mike Gold were chums in the early 1920s, when Sinclair looked upon young Gold, the romantic anarchist, as "one of the dearest fellows I ever knew, warmhearted and delightful, human." But to continue their friendship into the next decade might have indicated that he shared Gold's abysmal politics. He had, long ago. But those were the days before Gold turned Communist Party zealot and could affectionately castigate Upton, his "elder brother," for wincing at the earthy tastes and habits of the working class. All this and more I learned when Sinclair invited me to meet him.

That would be my second and last trip to Monrovia, where

my mother had died thirty-eight years before. Sinclair and his family were packing up to leave their smoggy city for Arizona when I got there, but he didn't seem at all put out by my arrival. Our interview began as soon as I stepped across the threshold of his house and into a dark room that contained only a few chairs, a standing lamp, and a table bearing a small figurine of Napoleon. Before answering my questions, he remarked on the package of cigarettes poking out of my coat pocket and pleasantly observed that surgeons would soon be cutting me up.

Van Wyck Brooks had dubbed Sinclair a "publicist," an apt term for someone who had written so effectively on so many controversial subjects. I didn't ask Sinclair about his pamphleteering, to what he attributed his vast readership in the USSR, or why he campaigned unashamedly for the Nobel Prize in literature, but I did learn from our impromptu chat that he disliked literary theorizing, ranked institutions higher than individuals on the evolutionary ladder, was "impatient with any form of human vanity or stupidity" and didn't easily forgive. After a half century, his feud with the Soviet director Sergei Eisenstein, into whose unfinished Mexican film he had sunk a lot of money, still rankled. (I was shocked when he told me that he had denounced Eisenstein as a libertine and swindler in a letter to Stalin and that Stalin had cabled back that he agreed.) I summarized Sinclair as a visionary immersed in hard facts, author of the 1928 *Boston* (still the best single account of the Sacco-Vanzetti case), secular evangelist, ascetic, and experimenter in strange diets, who deplored sensual indulgence as much as he did social injustice and dramatized his immunity from moral contamination.

Sinclair had moved to Pasadena in 1915. His novel *Oil!* (1926), with its background of Teapot Dome and the shenanigans of the Harding administration, is a panorama of Southern California civilization from 1912 to the mid-1920s: a blur of oil derricks, eucalyptus trees, corny road signs, speed traps, bungalows, faith healers, movie extravaganzas, and jokey advertisements. It evokes the

Los Angeles of my remembered boyhood more vividly than did the Los Angeles I was revisiting to interrogate the survivors of the old West Coast leftist literati.

Hollywood had been a port of call for Communist Party fund-raisers from the East Coast hoping to milk their sympathizers in the movie industry. Many of them had no jobs outside their party work and could be identified, it was said, by the make and age of their cars, but they knew how to play on the guilt of affluent screenwriters, whose weapons, Ernest Hemingway sneered, were the fountain pen and the typewriter. To get what they came for, they would prolong business meetings until the weary screenwriters sleepily retired and left the radical remnant to pass "correct" resolutions. This was known as "Democracy by exhaustion." At such gatherings, nonparty people often tended to be more ardently revolutionary than party members and readier to uphold the current Communist line.

Traces of the once-vociferous group of pro-Soviet writers were still visible and sometimes visitable in Los Angeles in 1957, but they were divided and scattered. A few had come back out of the cold after being fired or jailed, and some were camping in hospitable Mexico, to which American radicals and nonconformists had been fleeing for legal, financial, or political reasons since the days of Woodrow Wilson. Some of them were old friends of Joe Freeman and were embedded in the Mexican expatriate community. Joe urged me to see them while they were easily reachable. At the end of the Stanford session, I and Frank Barron, a fellow at the Center for Advanced Study in the Behavioral Sciences, flew to Mexico City, he to collect a batch of hallucinogenic mushrooms for his experiments on drugs and the creative process, I to pay some calls and gather information.

Our base was a small hotel hidden behind a wall that shielded the guests from the homeless families nearby. A gleaming limousine carelessly parked outside of the hotel and an Indian mother and her dirty-faced baby propped against one of its wheels signalized the two societies—the new rich and bedraggled poor—vividly and impersonally. In the next week, I saw comparable scenes enacted through the windows of taxis that carried me to my appointments.

Following Joe Freeman's instructions, I looked up his old friend Anita Brenner, an authority on Mexican art. A longtime resident of Mexico City, she had been an intimate of Orozco and Rivera among other Mexican painters, and it was she who told me how to reach the painter-adventurer David Siqueiros, who had organized and led a murderous assault against Trotsky. Semblances of the condottiere were visible in the soldierly man (a "boned pirate," as someone described Hawthorne) who invited me to his well-appointed house and gave me a good lunch. He had recently returned from a lecture trip to the Soviet Union, which, as a theoretical Communist, he still supported. I did not refer, nor did he, to Khrushchev's denunciation of Stalin at the Twentieth Congress of the Communist Party of the Soviet Union, but he pointedly mentioned his own critique of the official line on socialist realism as well as of the stodgy academicism and stylistic timidity of Soviet art. He thought even less well of abstract or nonrepresentational art fostered by rich American imperialists whom he accused of suborning talented, but vulnerable, painters like Rufino Tamaya. On aesthetic questions, he seemed closer to Trotsky, whom he had once tried to assassinate, than to Stalin.

After lunch, we drove to Chapultepec Castle in Siqueiros's Mercedes to inspect his unfinished mural, a vision of revolutionary Mexico crowded with soldiers, peasants, politicians, plutocrats, and rural police and littered with corpses. Then we drove to another mural project at a medical center, this project celebrating the triumph of medical science over cancer. It was a good day spent with a larger-than-life man as familiar with wars and prisons as he was with walls to paint on. Some months later, I learned that he had once again been jailed by the Mexican police.

VII

My search for writers and artists on the lam from congressional investigators continued in London, where a small number of blacklisted Hollywood exiles had found jobs writing and directing. Among them were humorist and screenwriter Donald Ogden Stewart (1894–1980) and his wife, Ella Winter, who had married the old muckraker Lincoln Steffens in her twenties. He had advised her to forget Stalin and Trotsky and to get at the ideas and policies of the Communist Party, and so she did. The Stewarts were living very comfortably in Hampstead in a fine house once owned by Ramsay MacDonald. From Hollywood they had transported their collection of Klees and Mondrians and other modern painters. So far as I could tell, Ella was unaffected by Khrushchev's disclosures at the Twentieth Congress of the Communist Party and was still an ardent Communist. She did her best to keep her pliant husband ideologically in line, but I don't think politics mattered to him any longer. He reminisced fondly about Yale in the 1920s, about the time he was kicked off the floor at a Smith College prom for improper dancing, and about his friends Scott Fitzgerald, Dos Passos, Hemingway, Gilbert Seldes, and Edmund Wilson. Apparently he had had little social consciousness in those days. I doubt very much that he had grieved over the fate of Sacco and Vanzetti or knew or cared about the radical sectarians. His antipathy toward Coolidge and Hoover, I gathered, had been less ideological than cultural. He didn't say how or when he became a Communist sympathizer, but he was still an "innocent," he told me, when he agreed to front for the Communist-dominated League of American Writers in later 1937. That was long ago, and he no longer felt any pressure to toe a political line. He seemed readier to recall his feckless youth than his time as a left-wing Hollywood impresario.

English ex-Communists didn't talk much about their own radical wild oats either, not because they feared being interrogated by some parliamentary committee on "un-English activities," but because they were inhibited by retrospective chagrin. In 1956, at the *Punch* office, the editor Malcolm Muggeridge, genial and steeped in bile, introduced me to the no-less-corrosive Claude Cockburn, whose dope sheet on Tory skullduggery I had subscribed to in the 1930s. "Tell Aaron about your Communist friends," Muggeridge urged him, and when Cockburn denied any such connections, Muggeridge compared him to an old whore who, after a long stay in a brothel, protested that she had never known what was going on. None of the lettered men of the Left whom I encountered in England had been "dedicated" Communist Party members, although a few of them, Wystan Auden and Stephen Spender, briefly thought of themselves as Communists. Neither, I noted, looked back with nostalgia or regret for his short ride on the "Red train."

I hadn't taken that particular excursion, but as a chronic radical democrat, I usually lined up with the disturbers of the peace and found it easy enough to lambaste American foreign or domestic policy. But then I began to notice that my periodic trips abroad coincided with moments when the United States was under fire for infringing the civil liberties of its own citizens or embroiled in unpopular foreign adventures. It was easy enough to lambaste on occasion American foreign and domestic policies when I was on my side of the Atlantic but harder while serving as a kind of unofficial diplomat abroad. Thus I found myself squirming with discomfort in London as I watched a performance of Bertold Brecht's *Threepenny Opera*. Sam Wanamaker, the American director and actor recently blacklisted by the House Un-American Activities Commitee, had scattered anti-American barbs throughout his production, quite in the spirit of Brecht but to me at once apposite and gratuitous. I could not bring myself to dump on Mother America, and this posed some problems.

The soul of Joseph McCarthy was still guttering while I investigated the impact of Communism on American writers and intellectuals; it did not totally fade after he died. Throughout the

Army-McCarthy hearings of 1954, the senator's face, which seemed impervious to razors, stared malignantly out of the television screen. It made you think, "Oh yes, it could happen here," given the ascendancy of well-heeled yahoos swollen with "passionate intensity" and on the hunt for enemies to finger and pursue.

PART SIX

The demonstrations popping up on American campuses in the 1960s
and extending to the 1970s began shortly after Joseph McCarthy's
unlamented death in 1957. They excited my sympathy and my vex-
ation. The underlying cause of student disquiet, I believed, was
the war in Vietnam, but its proclaimed target was the "establishment," the emerging bogey of what was to become an international youth estate. Liberals like me opposed American intervention in Southeast Asia, but many of us were also piqued by
student militants, with their strikes and nonnegotiable demands,
and by an officialdom that alternately over- and underreacted to
student dissent. True believers, on both the left and the right,
despised our tepid moderation. To the leftists under thirty and to
some of those over thirty as well, our kind of politics and culture
was out of date. Rude expletives once confined to walls and fences
had become commonplace in public discourse.

   I had spent a lot of time in the company of students in America and abroad and was probably less conscious of the age gaps
that divided "them" from "us" than were most people of my generation. I felt at ease with the rebellious young and wanted no part
in the looming generational fracas. I admonished myself: "Let the
young implode. Don't take sides or offer gratuitous advice." But
by the late 1960s, I lacked the patience and detachment to follow
this lofty counsel. I cringed from folksinging sessions where the
young and their elder gurus came to protest against the atomic

bomb, apartheid, and social discrimination or to enjoy their own theatricality, and I grew increasingly depressed by the displays of radical chic in fashion magazines and by the commercializing of causes. An older me had distanced himself from an earlier impulsive me and grown more receptive to codes and rules of behavior that I now believed made social intercourse less noisy and abrasive. Quotations in my journal circa 1968–70 leaned to the dry and the deflationary.

"Men will insist upon the universal application of a temporary feeling or opinion." (Melville to Hawthorne)
"The only thing the young people had definitely in common was the attack on objectivity, intellectual responsibility, and the balanced personality." (Robert Musil, *The Man without Qualities*)
"This atmosphere created by 'association' makes those who live in it 'devoid of responsibility and remorse,' to quote one of Kierkegaard's profound sayings in the dangers of shared activity." (Ellen Key, *The Younger Generation*)

Here was a problem: how to reconcile the generous social instincts of rebellious students with their bad manners and verbal brutalities ("Up against the wall, motherfucker!"). If I spoofed Victorian decorum, I was always startled when words and expressions that had been taboo when I was growing up were casually uttered in public discourse. Like many of my middle-aged friends and colleagues, I found myself reverting to the manners of my elders while still half convinced that the half-baked insurgents holding revivals and sit-ins on university campuses had some reason to believe, however simplistic their reasoning and violent their language, that we were bound to sell them out in the long run, hedge them in, douse their fires. "Every generation," the critic and reformer John Jay Chapman wrote a century ago, "is a secret society, and has incommunicable enthusiasms, tastes, and interests which are a mystery to its predecessors and to posterity."

That the so-called New Leftists and I were talking past each other became clearer to me after I chaired a debate titled "The

Old Left and the New" in 1967 at the Ninety-second Street YMCA. It pitted Dwight Macdonald and Richard Rovere, old vintage lefties, against two reigning junior Jacobins: Tom Hayden, then "resident activist" at Antioch College; and Ivanhoe Donaldson, well known on the radical student front for his "charisma." Neither Hayden nor Donaldson had bothered to read the list of questions put to them in advance or to spell out their positions in the debate. They used the occasion simply to scorch their opponents, whose flippant, but not ill-natured, animadversions ("those youngsters simply hadn't read enough") no doubt sounded insufferably patronizing. That Macdonald commended their idealism didn't matter. To these new stars of the political theater, eager to preach but not to listen, whatever the old geezers had to say was irrelevant. But then what to make of their own slogans and stratagems? What did "liberation" mean? Or "on strike?"

A second generational encounter happened in the next year (1968–69) at the University of Sussex, where I was about to teach and where I got my first prolonged look at the English Narodniki, priestly proud and melancholic. After I finished an informal talk on the coming American presidential election, a half-dozen members of my audience—all of them quick, articulate, and well informed—publicly challenged me. Why be "objective" and "fair," they asked, when confronting criminals of the establishment? Why grant them the freedom of the university grounds? Better to bait the intruders and pour ink on their heads, they concluded, even at the cost of ruffling a few civil liberties.

But if my liberalism was irrelevant—worse, a sellout to vested interests—it didn't seem so to me. At fifty-six, I felt duty-bound to reassert my loyalty to this unheroic tradition now under fire, especially after reading a passage of Hermann Hesse's *Steppenwolf* (1927), a novel that over the years had achieved among the youth estate a "How true!" status comparable to Thomas Wolfe's *Look Homeward, Angel* (1929) and Ayn Rand's oracular *The Fountainhead* (1943), which I facetiously reviewed in the *Partisan Review* without anticipating the imminence of a Rand cult. Hesse wrote of his hero: "No prospect was more hateful and distasteful to him than that he should have to go to an office and conform to daily and yearly routine and obey orders. He hated all kind of his offices, governmental or commercial, as he hated death, and his nightmare was confinements in barracks." Such sentiments sat very well with many student militants in 1968. They, too, scorned the middle-of-the-roaders who inhabited what Hesse called the "temperate zone." They loved "the political criminal, the revolutionary or intellectual seducer, the outlaw of the state and society." They abominated, as Hesse did, "the bourgeois liberal," a creature of weak impulses, neither saint nor profligate, anxious and fearful, and easy to rule—the patsy of the establishment.

II

An effervescent statement of the generational split that year was the production of a raucous, self-indulgent, and energetic musical happening that I saw in London after my run-in with the Sussex dissidents. *Hair* celebrated the stigmata of the youth revolt— beards and anarchic hair styles—and affirmed the holiness of the verbally and sexually forbidden, even though its collective message (directed primarily to the over-thirty population) came down to little more than "Fuck you, Square!" Throughout the performance, the theater was quite literally redolent of "grass," but not the sort that sent the ur-hippie Walt Whitman into space. Since age and conviction disqualified me from taking part in this rite of youth, as the audience was invited to do, I played the bemused onlooker unable to equate the celebrants' purity of spirit with the violence of their psychodramas, and I smugly contrasted what to me were *Hair*'s callow affirmations with the subversive asides of Emerson and Thoreau.

In England (as in American colleges then), a few elder and more than a few junior faculty members demonstrated their solidarity with the student come-outers. Quite literally, they let down their hair; they piously smoked pot at rock concerts and adopted the speech and accoutrements of the youth culture, much to the irritation of colleagues who disdained such overtures. Generational distinction was an ongoing theme in popular song lyrics, fiction, and movies, latent with meanings for symbol searchers and would-be cultural anthropologists. Thus, much could be made of a film I saw in Brighton cryptically titled *If,* a "romp" in the reviewer's jargon, but evocative of the convulsions brought on by the war in Vietnam, the "sexual revolution," and other happenings. I described *If* in my journal as a dark, comic fantasy set in a generic English public school, itself the antithesis of everything free, spontaneous, and uncorrupted. In *If,* authority figures incarnate repressive institutions, in sum the octopus establishment, but specifically the school, the church, and the military. Ranged against this integrated Moloch is a fresh-faced nihilist vanguard whose violent reprisals are justified by the malignity of their oppressors. A general and a bishop are rollickingly assassinated during a class-day ceremony toward the end of this murderous idyll. *If* vibrates with fun and guns, motorcycle rides and love wrestlings, but its message is sinister. "These kids," Henry Nash Smith wrote to me from Berkeley (6 Oct., 1969) "have a kind of purity that makes me feel as if I were the master mind of a dope and prostitution ring. Yet they talk of the most bloodthirsty psychodramas of revolution in a perfectly even tone of voice. No wonder Nixon can't understand them. I can't either."

Nothing comparably bloody ruffled the tranquility of Sussex or of any other English university in 1968–69—that is, nothing to match the student tumults in the United States or the disciplined takeover of university buildings by the predominantly socialist student body in Germany. Sussex had fewer combustible elements to contend with. Fifty-five percent of its students (a higher percentage than at Oxbridge) were technically upper-class, although you couldn't tell their social origins by their hair or beards. It was trendy to be leftish and working-class, but Sussex was politically apathetic, despite all of its splashing of paint on an

American embassy official and burning of flags of the United States and the United Kingdom to protest the imperialistic invasion of Vietnam.

Traditionally, American writers of English descent have had two minds about "Our Old Home," as Hawthorne called England. For him and for a number of other nineteenth-century Americans, the English were still distant cousins—although, since 1776, a condescending and justly resented ancestral foe. That's the way Edmund Wilson saw them. I asked him once why he was so hard on the English. He said it was because of the American Revolution, but that sounded rather far-fetched to me, unless he meant that the war had sundered a hitherto functioning cousinship. Wilson was a plainspoken and solidly educated man, quick to detect a solecism in the English language, written or spoken. It irked him when English writers (Virginia Woolf, for one) declared that English and American English were separate tongues. He passed over the sneering references to him and his country by such soi-disant aristos as Evelyn Waugh and Kingsley Amis as mischievous attempts to heat up old Anglo-American animosities. Yet he was not an ambassador of goodwill. That he had a large English following didn't stop him from dropping acerbic remarks about Albion. I had no such quarrel with England. It was too class-branded to qualify as my "great good place," but I was pleased to be in a country full of learned and tolerant people whose literature and history had once been more familiar to me than my own and the only country outside the United States where I had a clutch of abiding friends.

During that year at Sussex, the Lewes Literary Society asked me to fill in a lecturing engagement for the ailing literary journalist John Lehmann. My subject was the then little-known—and in my opinion greatest—American diarist George Templeton Strong (1820–75), who had carried on a lifelong irreverent affair with an England he never saw but whose literature and history he had absorbed. Pleased with the excerpts I quoted from Strong's wonderful four-volume diary, the society plunked down a hefty sum to buy it for their collection. Its president, Leonard Woolf, had been ill with the flu when I gave my talk, but he wrote me that he heard it had been "a great success" and invited me to Monk's House for dinner.

Woolf, a small thin man of eighty-eight with a deeply furrowed face and a smallish nose, presided over a very good dinner. There were four of us at table and two border collies in attendance. Negroes, Henry James, James Russell Lowell, the American Civil War, animals, G. E. Moore, Woolf's Ceylon, and two of Woolf's recently discovered cousins figured in the conversation. The last were the children of his delinquent Uncle Dan, his father's brother, who had forged a check and been hustled off to America to spare him punishment and shame. There he married a Roman Catholic woman, never telling his two children that he was Jewish; but they deduced as much after noting that a photograph of Leonard Woolf's father in his autobiography matched the one on their father's dresser. They were pleased to learn this fact, but relatives on their mother's side were not. Woolf was curious about this American connection (he had spent a few weeks in South Carolina) and asked me a lot of questions I couldn't answer about my own family history. Only once did the name of his wife, Virginia, come up in this evening of talk. It seemed, he mused, that a number of graduate students in the United States were writing their doctoral dissertations on her.

III

From elegant raffish Brighton, I followed the reports of the riots on American campuses and of student takeovers in German universities. Having spent a year in authentically authoritarian Poland, where protests and high jinks of any sort weren't indulged, I felt no urge to take part in the crusade against the establishment of which I was willy-nilly a part. Meanwhile, cynical observers at Berkeley, Columbia, Cornell, and other hot spots likened this great rebellion to the Children's Crusade or to a national revival meeting. A 1969 letter from a friend in California set the scene.

Every car, bike, window, garage door, garbage can has some kind of poster on it—"Remember the Pueblo," "Remember Chicago," "Dump the Hump," "Hitler is Alive and Campaigning for President," "Standup for America," "No!" "Send the Yippies to Vietnam," "MMM (Mao, Marx, Marcuse)," "Burn UC." It's a first-class Happening or a kind of Disney-cartoon version of the Russian Revolution. And the people here act like the posters. I attended one political rally at UCSD [University of California, San Diego]: full auditorium, 2000 on the lawns outside listening via loudspeakers, the place lined with what seemed like hundreds of cops. The climax of the speech was a chant set up by the candidate: "Fuck Reagan," repeated by the audience nine times (mystical number of the Black Panthers) and boomed by the amplifiers across the sunny plush town of La Jolla. Everyone turns red-faced and sweaty discussing the "issues" and they do nothing but that. Needless to say, the bête noire on all sides is the "liberal," the anachronistic dupe-humanitarian: dupe for the capitalist-fascist-imperialist or for the commie–anarchist–anti-American, depending on your point of view. To be young now in Southern California is very heaven.

Another sardonic correspondent described in similar terms a civil rights conference he had attended the same year. At this "quasi-religious event," as he described it, "the 'shoed or sandaled' communicants seemed to be following an unwritten script" and "groaned their applause at sporadic intervals." A week before, he had heard Stokely Carmichael preach to a receptive crowd in the University of Pittsburgh Student Union on the subject of the evils of "Western (so-called) Civilization." My correspondent reported that the audience "roared its approval at the thought of being guilty," while Stokely, "young, arrogant, handsome," pronounced integration a hoax, an evil spell. "Hurrah, we screamed," my correspondent concluded, "delighted to know how very rotten we were; even bourgeois Negro students were cheering their condemnation as rat finks."

Such dispatches made the eruptions on American campuses sound wilder than the student strikes I glimpsed on the Continent in the spring of 1969, while lecturing at a number of universities for the United States Information Service. I would pause at these academic way stations to speak on contemporary American writers, but not long enough to get much sense of the root cause of the disorders. European student activists were said to be older, better educated, and more mature than their American counterparts—less evangelical and less preoccupied by their own "identities." But I had no time to test this hypothesis. In Hamburg, students were on strike, and even the America House located within the university proper showed some broken windows. Signs and notices and belligerent proclamations festooned university buildings inside and out. On "captured" floors, students occupied the offices of professors whose names on office doors had been crossed out with red crayons or ink and whose desks were strewn with beer bottles. Clarion announcements evinced the determination of the strikes to hold firm ("We Shall Conquer" or "The Talking Period Is Over—Now Battle") and to resist authority ("*De Gaulle est un con*"). Everyone appeared to be calm and polite. Only the objurgations on the walls were violent. Not until late in the morning did I learn that my lecture on Norman Mailer would proceed on schedule. Some forty to fifty came to hear me out, not, very likely, because I pointed out analogies between *The Naked and the Dead* and *Moby Dick*, but because they may have perceived in Mailer's novel themes they thought pertinent to the strike.

I left Hamburg with only a vague notion of what the strike was really about and not much inclined to side with either the domineering professoriat or the posturing protesters. Here was a country in which, it was said, an "artful and militant few" could capture a movement by rigging procedures, packing meetings, monopolizing loudspeakers, and stifling majority opinion, as the first steps toward smashing the universities and disestablishing the establishment. Decades before, H. L. Mencken—the famous American editor and critic—had compared college nihilists in New York City during the Depression to kittens trying to upset the Matterhorn, but for a short time, German students unnerved the officials trying to quash them. A charwoman was heard to say, "If Hitler were here, these student strikes wouldn't last a minute." They did last, however—until the movement deconstructed.

Before returning to Brighton, I read an article in an American magazine chiding "liberal moderates" for failing to grasp that in an irrational society, it is rational to shout and protest and disobey. But what if the "irrational society" happened to be a police state as well, where student dissidents were clubbed and jailed? Once again while on the road for the USIA in the spring of 1969, I had occasion to consider that question.

Queens University, Belfast—the site of a UK American studies conference—was my unlikely takeoff point, an island of sanity insulated from the bullhorn roars of Reverend Ian Paisley and the sounds of his surly antipapist Orangemen in the Stormont Parliament House. I wasn't sad to exchange Belfast for Belgrade, my doorway to Yugoslavia. During the next five days, I talked about American books in Novi Sad, Sarajevo, Zagreb, and Ljubljana. Later trips to these places would deepen and correct first impressions, but in 1969, I declared the Yugoslav universities to be, if not bastions of freedom, the freest in Central Europe. Whether this was true or not, I didn't realize then that young Yugoslavians had greater cause to worry about their future in a country pulled to pieces by rival nationalisms than to fear and resent their oppressive elders. As I was to feel even more positively in subsequent trips to Serbia, Croatia, and Slovenia, the student population was the most ecumenical element in Yugoslavia's six republics, although not strong and pervasive enough to still the religio-political tensions between the Yugoslavian "nations" in the post-Tito era. Here, as in Poland and Romania, there were few legitimate vents for spontaneous political expression. This obvious fact became all the more obvious in Warsaw, where, arriving after a five-day interlude in Rome, I learned from Polish friends how government paramilitaries had corrected student misbehavior with truncheons in the previous year.

The euphoria that lingered faintly a decade after Khrushchev's disclosures at the Twentieth Congress of the Communist Party of the Soviet Union was gone by the spring of 1969. On my taxi drive from the grubby Warsaw airport to the city center, I saw lines of trucks loaded with uniformed men on the side streets. The days of comparative relaxation and gaiety appeared to be over: student outbursts in March 1968 had been more intense and more savagely repressed than reported in the West. I heard a number of eyewitness accounts of this business—how vodka-soused irregulars had entered hitherto privileged university space and roughed up the students, not sparing the intransigent sons and daughters of Communist Party officials. The government, it was said, had been scared by the boldness of the student demonstrations— hence its fierce retaliation. When I arrived, the campaign against Jews and the friends of Jews was still in swing, the devious General Mieczyslaw Moczar running the show.

Long talks with embittered friends enlarged this dismal and paradoxical chronicle. I reported in my journal that the witty and charming and now understandably morose Mrs. K., a former colleague, received obscene phone calls orchestrated by the secret police day and night. Her lover, a well-known Jewish novelist, was constantly being notified that his "whore" or "bitch" was consorting with other men. One of Mrs. K.'s longtime friends and supporters—a brilliant, kooky scholar with whom I'd once had friendly, if gingerly, relations—was said to back Moczar's anti-Semitic policies, but qualifiedly. While he favored purging the Jews from the English department that he now headed, he refused to collaborate with the police against its tainted members. When they were kicked out, he sent them flowers (not cynically, either); and he attended their funerals. Students considered him paranoid and demonic and reported that when he was in an ugly mood, his red eye glared like the Devil's. "They call me *starry* [old one]," he complained to me bitterly, and he warned Mrs. K. that I spied for the Central Intelligence Agency.

According to a department member about to lose her job, half of her university colleagues, including Mrs. K.'s friends and mine, were political spies; and she went on to elaborate on Moczar's tactics—how he posed as the guardian of artists and the young while backing the invasion of Czechoslovakia. Once, she said, he could and ought to have been exposed as a police spy. It was too late now, she lamented: everyone distrusted everyone; Poland was a fascist country. This gloomy picture was in my mind when I accepted the department's coldly correct invitation to address an audience of professional brass and inhibited students. Apparently there had been a big to-do about my coming, and the chairman introduced me correctly, but without warmth, as a former associate. I knew there would be a long hiatus before my next show.

The presupposition of my Warsaw hosts that I was a CIA spy may have accounted in part for my chilly reception there. However far-fetched, it became more comprehensible to me a month later, after a weekend in Paris with a recently exiled Polish couple. We had become good friends in Warsaw five years before. Both were Polish-born Jews who had spent their adolescence in Brazil, and both were university teachers—she a member of the English faculty and he a widely traveled expert on the economics of developing countries. They had been expelled from Poland during the anti-Semitic campaign of Moczar and company, a campaign touched off by the Israeli-Arab Six Days' War. While Paris was churning with police and demonstrators, I heard the story of their expulsion.

It had all happened pretty quickly, although my friends were surprised to learn how long Moczar and his "Partisanki" had been conniving against them. During the past four years, they had bugged the economist husband's conversations as far afield as a Mexican airport when he was away on government business, provoked the student uprising that brought hyped-up goons into the university grounds, persuaded Gomułka for a time that "revisionists" and "Zionists" (that is, Jews) had egregiously celebrated the defeat of the Arabs, and urged him to take the darkest view of a meeting at which my friend and some of his fellow technocrats had projected plans to improve socialist efficiency. After four hours of insulting interrogation, replete with calculated slurs about his "race," he was given two weeks to settle his affairs (namely, sell or give away what he would have to leave behind) and clear out. This final humiliation neither changed his political philosophy nor curdled his memories of fair-minded neighbors, shopkeepers, and casual acquaintances who, though, hardly philo-Semitic, took pains to do favors for him and his wife and to treat them with respect.

I flew from Warsaw to Bucharest in one of the comfortable gooselike LOT planes favored by the Poles. Three Polish officers (two colonels and a general), unbuttoned and noisy, were on board, and during the meal served immediately after takeoff, they opened a bottle of vodka and began to swallow half tumblers at a gulp. Two hard-featured women (*babkas*) near me joined the ad hoc party and shortly were being pawed by their hosts while the other passengers pretended not to notice. Bucharest looked Mediterranean after the cold Warsaw fog.

The Romanian Writers Union sponsored this rather pointless junket, not the University of Bucharest, although I was scheduled to speak there as well. The two groups couldn't be more different—the university's professors of English Anglophilic and academically correct, the writers (largely poets, novelists, playwrights, translators, and editors) of the bohemian persuasion. The latter were making the most of a temporary thaw (the atmosphere reminiscent of Warsaw six or seven years before) and feeling secure enough to skewer the Russians, if not their local masters. But hopes of liberation, high in 1964, had dwindled by 1968. Contacts with foreigners were strictly monitored. There was no place to talk to my hosts in unsupervised surroundings or to meet informally with students who showed up at my lectures and vanished. On April 16, 1969, I wrote in my journal:

Went to a performance of *Carmen*. Judging by the half-filled house, opera isn't a passion here, although dozens of other reasons might account for the small attendance. Don José sung by an "honored artist of the USSR" with a Georgian name, a square man who looked like a squashed Victor Mature. Sung well, at times beautifully, but no taste. I enjoyed the opulent multichinned Carmen. She swished seductively, a rose clenched in her teeth, and made the scenery quake.

In Bucharest, I saw a performance of a dramatic parable whose fine points were beyond me, yet it was recognizably anti-Soviet. Afterward, at a gathering of artists and intellectuals, I met a fat, tough, bibulous roaring dog just back from Russia. He talked about American writers (he'd read quite a lot of them) and lectured to me on what it meant to be a Romanian, intellectually and politically. Obviously, an unscarred visitor from the United States couldn't conceive of what it was like to live under an impending avalanche, but he and his pals had no illusions about life in the police state where spies and philistines degraded the artists. In his opinion, Americans were soft, Russians hard. He argued that world opinion wouldn't deter the Russians (although the People's Republic of China might) from descending on Romania. If they did, he said, they would be pelted not with flowers, as they were by the ignoble Czechs, but with Molotov cocktails. (Nicolae Ceauşescu's name was conspicuously unmentioned in this alcoholic farrago.)

I left Bucharest with impressions of a muzzled society but with no sense of what was going on beneath its agreeable-enough surface. More unregulated talk might have corrected or qualified an ungenerous hunch that the cowed citizens accepted restraints on their civil liberties more philosophically than they did the constraints on their pleasures. The students I talked to loved their land but not to the point of wasting five years of their youth in the boondocks, where admittedly their skills were desperately in demand. They wanted to earn more money and to live better and to share in the international youth culture (films, music, clothes) available in the latitudinarian West. Their interest in America and the American language seemed to have little to do with the politically illicit or the intellectually arcane. It just happened that the English of American popular songs and movies was becoming the lingua franca of a multinational generational culture more averse to dullness than to tyranny. These and kindred unwarranted notions occurred to me en route from Bucharest to Berlin. Everywhere, the trusty dichotomies—rich and poor, haves and have-nots—had melted into "them" and "us." The protesters who shut down universities or charged police cordons or rioted in countries where they weren't likely to be beaten up or hauled off to jail belonged, more often than not, to the middle class. Their collective antipathy was directed against the force or forces constituted to break them in, seduce them into a system, coerce them into conformity.

In Berlin, I read *They* (1920), a dark comedy by the Polish painter and writer Stanisław Ignacy Witkiewicz, about the successful conspiracy of an antilife agency to eliminate the individual, the personal, the unpredictable. "They" (the League of Absolute Automationism) is covertly in command as the play opens, the opposition already corrupted and denatured. In subsequent grotesque scenes, the conspirators step out of their former bogus simulated selves and complete the conquest. In the world of "They," art is in the process of being monopolized by the decadent dilettantes—soft, infantile anarchists who, uncreative themselves, have drained the creativeness of others. The ideal state for these impotent vampires is the permissive society that encourages the rebel to push art to the extreme of madness and perversion and thus smooth the way for the repressive totalitarian mechanists waiting in the wings.

IV

Witkiewicz's fable prompted musings of pandemic violence, but Smith College in the fall of 1968 was tranquil as usual, and Harvard University, to which I was about to return after a thirty-year hiatus, was untroubled by violence. Elsewhere, too, educational institutions appeared to be less combustible than they were a few years earlier. When I visited the People's Republic of China in the spring of 1980, the Cultural Revolution of the late sixties was history, even though its reverberations were still palpable.

Every survivor or victim or witness had a tale to tell, and there was little sympathy I could discover for the youthful hordes unleashed by Chairman Mao and then belatedly repressed—only anger and shock at their mindless destructiveness. My informants were mostly academics and their families, a number of whom had been sent to be reeducated in the country (namely, to live with peasants in mud huts, take care of pigs, and, as it sometimes happened, eat bark and grass). So far as I could gather, few of them came out of this experience with Tolstoyan insights about themselves or their society. The men and women stigmatized for a few years as "stinking intellectuals" and "capitalist roaders" emerged from their ordeal content to abide by traditional stratifications. They pointedly distinguished themselves from peasants and workers and applauded the downfall of the Gang of Four and the arrest of Mao's widow, Jian Qing. Back in China in 1981, as I watched on television as she was removed from courtroom to prison, I heard a disdainful critic sum her up as an imperious and revengeful romantic, more stupid than wicked, whom a senile Mao protected until his death. Her favorite novels were said to be *The Count of Monte Cristo* (because the hero gets even with the men who framed him) and *Gone with the Wind* (because she was fan of Clark Gable).

The middle-aged and elderly I spoke to in the PRC may have been frightened and angered by Mao's young disciples, but in 1980, they struck me as oddly incurious about what lay behind the brief and explosive mass insurrection. It was enough for them that the dethroned had been restored and that the rampaging Red Guards had been sent back to the hinterlands. Keeping order everywhere were the troops of the People's Liberation Army, in their unnatty uniforms. On May 13, 1980, two of them escorted me around a military museum in Beijing, one reciting in Chinese the story of the PLA's heroic achievements, the other repeating the same in English. Both speakers might have stepped out of a propaganda poster. Their memorized script was sprinkled with references to "gangs," "imperialists," and "reactionaries," and the photographs on display testified to the courage and humanity of the Red Army: there were photos of an officer placing his great-coat on the backs of two sleeping soldiers, of peasant farmers and soldiers cultivating a field together, of a company of troops bivouacking in the streets lest they disturb civilian households. Other exhibits documented Japanese atrocities in Nanking and the more recent outrages committed by the Vietnamese. The latter's incursions, one of the guides sternly declared, had been smashingly rebuffed.

Noticeably missing from the PLA chronicle were references to the Cultural Revolution and, of course, to the enormities of the Red Guards. In a society where filial disrespect was once an unforgivable sin, young disciples of Mao had trashed "bourgeois" amenities (books, furniture, art, phonograph records), publicly humiliated their seniors, forced teachers to wear dunce caps, and hounded some of them to suicide. (These were the days when telephone callers had to say "Long live Chairman Mao" or the party at the other end would hang up.) With the rustication of the Red Guards, the era of disorder ostensibly ended. Mao Zedong, four years dead in 1980, was still an icon in a troubled society, his bland face, together with the familiar visages of Marx, Lenin, and Stalin, gazing down in Tianamen Square. But the enormous statues of him scattered ad nauseam in parks and squares were thinning out when I reached Beijing. Their quiet removal was said to have no political import, but it presaged his gradual demotion.

Gossip about Mao Zedong's despotic acts and unseemly appetites encouraged ignorant and imaginative foreigners like me to look for analogues in Chinese history and legend. I fancied I found them in tales of virtuous and wicked emperors and their retinue of ministers, generals, and concubines. The good among them were likely to be wrongheaded and gullible as well as loyal. The bad, enmeshed in betrayals and murders (often by poisoning and strangulation), unwittingly connived with their destroyers. The behavior of the gods of Chinese legend was also unexemplary. Their interventions could be as cruel as they were excessive. All of this violent lore (the stuff of Peking opera, to which I quickly became addicted) blended suggestively with the rumored skullduggeries in the court of "Emperor" Mao Zedong and supplied me with an endless dumb show for episodes in my private history of the PRC—including the Cultural Revolution. On June 10, 1980, I wrote in my journal:

My last Peking opera, *The Great Secret of Being Equal to the Gods,* one of many episodes about the Monkey King, a Chinese legend of especial charm for children. The Monkey King had been assigned a job in heaven—to guard the Garden of Peaches. (Just one bite of these peaches guarantees immortality to the biter.) He feels very important until he finds out that the gods haven't invited him to their banquet. Incensed, he crashes the party, eats up all the peaches, drinks all the wine, and goes on a cosmic rampage. The Monkey King (mischievous and comical but also strong and brave) and his monkey troops defeat the heavenly emperor's soldiery. Subdued at last and sentenced to death by burning, he pops out of the oven stronger than ever. The emperor beseeches Buddha to tame the obstreperous rebel, which he finally does, but not before the monkey army has routed a grotesque crew of drunken, misshapened, squabbling monks.

v

By the 1970s, the youth rebellion in the West had been institutionalized and commercialized, and its "Monkey Kings" had been brought to heel. The end of the Vietnam War quieted the campuses in the United States, now that young men no longer had to flee the country to escape the draft or devise ingenious stratagems to weasel out of it. Rioting ceased in Germany and France, and a momentary decline in repressive regimes elsewhere calmed potential troublemakers.

Radical movements, I decided, differed from country to country depending on the latitude permitted by the state. Security and prosperity made for tolerance; democracy, real or feigned, looked—and usually was—more conducive to freedom than was autocracy, for the agreed-on assumptions of a society, even when contradicted by fact, aren't meaningless. Rich countries tend to be more indulgent than poor ones, laxer in the enforcement of rules, slower in cracking down on the extravagancies of the young. So it is with countries whose histories are engrained with traditions of civil liberty.

That the multinational tumults in the 1960s were an electrical response of the under-thirty age-group to the injustice, cruelty, and hypocrisy of their elders is very doubtful, despite the protesters' ringing manifestos. A more probable cause, in the United States at least, was the Vietnam War and fear of the draft. Protests stopped with the war's end. In his poem "To a Political Poet," Tom Paulin alludes to the domestication of the hitherto dangerous and out-of-bounds: "Now your whinges / Get taught in classes / And the kids feel righteous—/ Righteous but cozy."

The public may have not have given Gerald Ford his due, but I don't think it misjudged him as it did James Earl Carter Jr., a more ambiguous phenomenon. Neither likable nor dislikable, the thirty-ninth U.S. president was an anomaly and hard to slot. Edmund Wilson's wife, Elena, was the first of my friends to support his candidacy. She gave me a Carter campaign button to wear when Massachusetts voters had barely heard of him. I remained an unwavering, if lukewarm, supporter throughout his accident-prone term, despite what I took to be his Baptist pieties.

I've never learned when or why Carter dropped his given name for the boyish "Jimmy." Maybe he thought it sounded less starchy and buttoned-up, but in my opinion "Jimmy" doesn't suit him; he's not a chummy man. Nor was this twice-born believer with Jesus's initials a "Christer" umbilically attached to the religious right. He did not feign his religiosity like so many attenders of prayer breakfasts. He looked cold and reserved on occasion, but not smug. His mirthless smile and the wintry glint in his eye struck me as more authentic than his flashes of kindly warmth.

Inveterate anti-GOPsters like me stuck with him when he was nearly drowning under a cascade of crises he had not anticipated and could not handle. Miscalculations and bad luck did him in. His reluctant decision to grant asylum on medical grounds to the shah of Iran inflamed the Khomeini revolutionists. So did the bungled tactical military mission in 1980 to spring the American hostages in Tehran. These disasters, together with a lot of economic bad news, sapped the confidence of even zealous Carterites and rationalized the attacks of his vilifiers.

I had been haphazardly aware of U.S.-Iranian relations since the CIA intervened in Iran (1953) and replaced the uncooperative Mohammed Mossadegh with the pliable pro-Western regime of the shah. In 1975, a week's stay at the University of Shiraz gave me more than an inkling of the depth and breadth of student hostility toward the shah. Those with whom I had covert conversations poured out stories about the enormities of SAVAK, the shah's secret police, and about how it spotted, tortured, and disposed of troublemakers. In nearby Persepolis, I saw some light-flooded ruins of ancient Persia and the so-called City of Tents the shah had had expensively erected to celebrate Iran's glorious past and himself. In a reception line there, I was presented to his wife (a good-looking pleasant woman) as a visiting Turk. She was trailed by a flunky who held out a tray to catch cigarette ashes she flicked out as she talked. These experiences in a country where repressiveness and brutality were heaving just below the surface of Iranian daily life no doubt colored my ambivalent response to the events that undermined Carter's administration.

Persepolis was far away and exotic, but at least it was a place I had seen. For many years, Plains, Georgia, was simply Jimmy

Carter's home address—and no less remote. I still preferred him to some admittedly more popular and effective presidents, but I took no interest in his roots or personal history until Ronald Reagan, battening on Carter's inflation problems and his failure to spring the American hostages in Tehran, sent him packing to his peanut farm. Thereafter, it was not so much what Carter did as what he didn't do that appealed to me: he shunned the role of the self-memorializing, golfing, party sage. It could be that his elaborately inconspicuous good works, his popping up in unwholesome places, his monitoring of dicey elections, and his "kindly carpenter" persona were more self-serving than they appeared to be. Perhaps they were canny spiritual investments. Anyway, he looked pretty good to me dressed in his overalls, standing on a ladder, sawing planks, painting clapboards, and pounding nails.

Nothing Carter wrote or said is likely to be engraved in stone. He seems somehow outside the presidential procession—or, rather, he floats above it like the grin of the Cheshire cat. I think both his well-wishers and his ill-wishers might agree with the summation that Carter was strong, intelligent, and honorable; that he had only a few major successes; and that he meant well.

Shortly before the end of President Reagan's second term, I blurted out to an astonished historian—just named (unbeknownst to me at the time) the president's authorized biographer—that Ronald Reagan was an odious man and a bad president. I knew less about him than I did about James K. Polk, but that didn't stop me from pegging Reagan as a shill for the corporate interests and the mouthpiece for the Republican radical Right. Subsequent reading and inquiry brought him into slightly sharper focus, contextualized him, shamed my intemperate and unbuttressed canards, but left my antipathy intact. On July 19, 1985, I wrote in my journal:

The Times reports a device concocted by a scientist in the Agriculture Department to detect "larval infestation." Based on the principle of the seismograph, it can record the sounds of maggots chewing away on a grapefruit, mangoes, apples, walnuts, peaches. We need a similar stethoscopic instrument to detect the larval infestation in government bureaus, particularly the maggots of the "diptera reaganesis" implanted in the body politic already riddled by these costly and destructive insects.

It was depressing to acknowledge what had long been evident to less-inflamed minds—that Ronald Reagan was politically adept and very popular. Liberals and intellectuals, often the butt of his mechanical witticisms, might lump him (as I did) indiscriminately with the hot GOPsters, but he appealed to a broad aggregate in both parties. Voters, put off a little by Barry Goldwater's truculence, felt easier with the jokey, genial Reagan dressed in the raiment of Uncle Sam. They also identified him with the Marlboro Man, whose cowpuncher image he traded on, and with the fellow next door who lends you a shovel or helps you change a tire. They were behind him when he slapped down the striking air controllers. They stayed loyal to him, if not to all the Reaganite programs and tactics, and comfortable with a commonsensical politician who didn't bluster and who was touchingly attached to his wife. On May 30, 1981, I wrote in my journal:

> At Waterville, Maine, Colby College, the usual festivities but in heavy rain. Meet Garry Trudeau, creator of *Doonesbury* and the graduating seniors' choice for their class speaker. His witty talk, autobiographical and political, was the highlight—his target, the Reagan administration. Sitting next to each other as the students came up to collect their diplomas, we invented a game: try to guess a student's major before it is announced, simply on the basis of his or her dress, walk, expression.

I had joined the Smith College faculty the same year that Nancy Davis, Mrs. Reagan-to-be, arrived in Northampton. Most of her classmates came with the same anti-Roosevelt credentials, but their orthodoxy tended to etiolate as they matured.

Nancy Davis's did not. Thanks to her stepfather's spiritual medications, she proved immune to the radical virus floating in the campus air, and her antipathy to leftist/liberal doctrine had only deepened by the time she met Reagan in filmland. Some of his commentators even believe it was she who accelerated his course Republicanward and transformed her uxorious and grateful spouse from gentle Democrat and hero-worshiper of FDR into militant Manichaean and archfoe of the "evil empire" of the Soviet Union.

In my skewed vision, the Reagan presidentiad is a sequence of events directed by RWR, master of ceremonies. It is also a bedraggled Hollywood epic that begins with the hero's birth in Tampico, Illinois, and fades away in 1988, when he passes out of public circulation. During his interim in the limelight, he's still hard to grasp and hold, enwrapped in his successive selves: youthful churchgoer waiting for Armageddon, conscientious lifeguard, sports announcer (vivifier of what he hasn't seen), movie actor internalizing the roles he's played, voice of General Electric, governor of California, president of the United States. Subsuming them all is the man I have transmogrified into a carrier of an endemic national disease.

Political attitudes aren't genetically determined, but most of us are weaned on the prejudices of our elders. Their opinions, like ours, were influenced not only by where they got their "corn pone" (as Mark Twain put it) but also by unrecognized imponderables. At our coming-of-age, whether politically engaged or not, we incline toward one party or political philosophy rather than another, so my slant on Reagan's vice president, George Herbert Walker Bush, was probably predictable. Had I kept a political hit list, he might have been condensed as follows: "Carefully nurtured beneficiary of old Republican gentry, other-directed rather than inner-directed, and drawn tropistically to power. Hence his 'ready versatility of conviction' (Veblen) and readiness to affiliate with hard-liners of Texas and elsewhere. Counters the 'wimp' charge by talking tough ('kicking ass') to ingratiate himself with ruffians and kooks although clearly not one of them."

Bush swam into my orbit at the start of the 1987 presidential campaign that pitted Reagan's heir against Michael Dukakis. For several months, I and a few other early risers had been talking politics with the Massachusetts governor in George Papalimberis's barbershop off Harvard Square whenever our haircuts coincided. Papalimberis, justly respected for his sagacious political judgment, presided over our session. Should "the Duke" compete in the presidential sweepstakes? Was this the right moment? Those were the central questions. The drama unfolded in my journal.

December 24, 1986: Up early, ate breakfast fast, and dashed to the barbershop. Got there just before George arrived. Three of us in the shop: George, a Panamanian (smart and well read), and me. We discuss Reagan, Bush, the Republican Party, and Governor Dukakis. The Panamanian keeps referring to me as "this gentleman." He had predicted that Mike would make a comeback and beat Ed King, who had whipped him in the last race for governor. Now he observes that Mike might get the Democratic presidential nomination. Enter the governor (one of George's old customers) at this precise moment. It's fate, says the Panamanian: we'll never forget this day. Dukakis remembers me from the Northampton days when our kitchen was a meeting place for visiting pols. He seems relaxed and confident as he explains to the Panamanian why an administrator might not always know what his aides are up to.

May 22, 1987: Another barbershop seminar with "the Duke." Again a Norman Rockwell setting with Dukakis chatting away about the futility of polls, but he's obviously pleased that the *Los Angeles Times* calls him a front-runner in spite of his recent litany on TV that there aren't any leading candidates and won't be for a long time. Says he really enjoys campaigning and is glad he entered the race no matter what the outcome. Acts jaunty and confident. I ask him if he's read Francis Fitzgerald's piece on the Sunbelt evangelicals around Reagan and their cult song of "I Love America." Told him I considered that song the anthem of the American nativists and that I much preferred "Columbia, the Gem of the Ocean." He said he didn't feel this way himself but added that the U.S. had been a model for younger republics, including Greece. Invited me to feed any suggestions I might have to his "idea man," a former Swarthmore classmate. George Papalimberis is very pleased with his barbershop forum.

February 16, 1988: Re the New Hampshire primaries: Dukakis on top, but I fear for him in the South. Bush said to be a more vulnerable opponent than Dole, but I don't think so. My guess: Bush plus money plus the imprimatur of Reagan (still unaccountably popular) plus materialism of the voters are likely to elevate a disingenuous weak man to "the greatest office in the world" and grease the glissade of the nation.

In the privacy of my closet, I made a pretense of being disinterested, but several entries in my journal show that I either weakly contested or yielded entirely to my biases: "Bush's convention address contrived as all get-out. Here and there a whiff of sincerity but mostly a pastiche of GOPisms with a touch of William Graham Sumner's 'The Forgotten Man'" (August 18, 1988); "Caught tail end of Dan Quayle's credo, a vacuous summation of his grandmother's injunction to accomplish what you set out to do. Sounded like a high school valedictorian address. He talked about his 'speriences'" (August 5, 1988); "Heard snippets of Bush inaugural. Music behind his heartfelt and empty words hinted of generous condescension. He will be the 'steward' in the Puritan sense, serving God by serving God's people. The hypocrisy and impudence of the Republican sales pitch—the crassest materialism couched in the cant of scoundrels" (January 20, 1989).

I concluded that Governor Dukakis lost to a well-intentioned, if occasionally unscrupulous, politician who had quashed his liberal propensities for a time in order to placate the ultraright wing of his party; that Bush's ambitions had outsoared his talents; that few presidency seekers (with the possible exception of John Quincy Adams) had had comparable opportunities to prepare themselves for the job; that Bush lacked the essential stuff (self-assurance, imagination, intellect) to rise above the lower echelons of presidents; that, standing on the world stage with his famous and infamous contemporaries (Nixon, Reagan, Margaret Thatcher, Saddam Hussein), he didn't bulk large enough even in his few triumphant moments; and that he was effaced by scouring events.

That could not be said of William Jefferson Clinton, whose name, obscure before 1989, would soon be in the history books. He was born William Jefferson Blythe (apposite surname), thirty-four years after my own birth date. A prophetic artist would have painted good and bad angels hovering over the infant's crib.

Americans have grown accustomed to Clinton's cheerful mug and Arkie intonations (the slightly querulous rise of his spoken sentences), have forgiven his youthful experiments in pot smoking and his alleged draft-dodging maneuvers (Vietnam was never a hallowed war), and have enjoyed his cheerfulness and élan. At first, he looked too beamish to speak for "the greatest nation on earth" and out of place on battleships or consorting with army brass, but soon he showed that his deal-cutting shrewdness acquired on the Arkansas hustings belied his boyishness. He was one of those beefy, vascular men Emerson (with reservation) marveled at: a man of size, weight, energy, "who knows men, can talk well on politics, trade, law, war, and religion." Such men, Emerson said, want power, "not candy." W. J. Clinton wanted both.

The last president of the century stumbled and nearly broke his neck in the first part of his second term. Like the dark-browed Nixon, he became the butt of cartoonists, writers, and media pundits. Yet to the rage and consternation of his enemies, he survived the firestorm he'd ignited, badly burned but still viable. How could that be? Anti-Clintonians ascribed the miracle to Clinton "fool-luck" or Clinton "spin." They had seen to it that the story of his appalling behavior be unsparingly told (even at the risk of polluting the innocence of America's children). And so it was, again and again, but without the expected political consequences. The voters seemed to be more curious than shocked, and the tarnished president remained acceptable to a solid bloc of the electorate.

Bill Clinton's dereliction broke into the course of the nation's business and made the easygoing chief executive, his steely-handsome wife, his college-student daughter, his quondam mistress, and his spooky chief prosecutor the characters in an American morality play. Our president had entangled himself in a preposterous "relationship" with a silly young woman and thereby delivered himself into the hands of a pious rabble who declared themselves betrayed. Untold numbers were genuinely affronted by the president's wrigglings and tergiversations. Prosecutors turned persecutors delightedly uncovered debris from his careless past. In some instances, it seemed to me that their obvious pleasure in collaring and disgracing a "rogue" far exceeded their professed pain in having to disclose his iniquities. It was the old American story, most famously told by Nathaniel Hawthorne: the zealous harassers of sin and hypocrisy are themselves transformed into monsters. Around this time, I wrote in my journal:

A few months ago, I heard a musical satirist entertain members of the Washington Press Club with some not very comical blackguardisms having to do with "servicing" the president. At last you can sing or say practically anything (unless offensive to gender or race) with impunity so long as your target is the Antichrist. Has any other president had his sexual transgressions so relentlessly and minutely aired? (Jefferson? Harding? JFK?)

My Bill Clinton (no doubt remote from the real article) is a puzzle, an uncommon "common man," an actor in the Tom Sawyer sense—that is, a romantic who has a high capacity for fun yet keeps his eye on the main chance and anchors his day-dreams on hardpan. His well-documented prevarications are boyish—hence his sobriquets "Slick Willie" and the "Comeback Kid." The key word is *kid*, an appellation that fits no other American president. This Bill Clinton irritates and alarms his foes and is hard to scotch. His mind is capacious and well stocked with retrievable information. He speaks with confidence and clarity. There's more Jefferson in him than Washington, more Van Buren's fox than Jackson's hickory, more of FDR than of Abraham Lincoln, yet he is not really like either (although, like both of them, he is a crafty man). He relishes presidential pomp, the privilege to spread American largesse and, if necessary, to dispatch bombers. His term is past its end, but in the new century, he's not likely to hide his head in a basket. 🐝

AFTERMATH

I

I initially wrote the preceding parts of this book in 1997. Seven years later at midpoint in the presidentiad of Clinton's successor—not a propitious time for the Republic—I take stock of my own history without pretending to understand its jerky course. At post-ninety, I have less to conceal than I did when I was twenty, and I look back at the years I've lived through, if not complacently, at least with relief that I've managed to escape hanging. It is no longer part of my job to be a professional "Americanist," a term until now I've always shunned. Even to pose as one in 2007 would daunt me.

In the 1940s and 1950s, the words *American* and *un-American* resonated in public speech. Such topics as the "American character" and the "American mind" slipped into academic discourse. One learned that to be an American was a "complex fate" (without quite understanding what Henry James meant by that cryptic phrase), and I wondered at times just what was so peculiarly "American" about America. The Frenchman Crèvecoeur asked that question when Americans were still British subjects but, according to him, already "a strange mixture of blood" not to be found in any other country. Did being "American" mean that one's family had to have lived for generations in the States? I knew people who believed as much. If so, how long did it take before one was sufficiently rooted in American soil to qualify as an authentic American? Who decided? Were the superchauvinists among the recent hyphenates overcompensating for their recency? Was the quintessential "American" amalgam of all races and nations and the United States an Amazonian flood "made up of a thousand noble currents all pouring into one" (to use Herman Melville's watery metaphor)?

Such questions no longer preoccupy me. Whether I like it or not, I am part and parcel of the country I sprouted from and lived in and studied. Although I no longer try to keep up with the prodigious amount of popular and scholarly writing published under the vague rubric of the ever-expounding and boundaryless "American studies," I am embedded in the USA.

In his autobiography, Benjamin Franklin defines a "reasonable creature" as one who finds or makes a reason "for everything one has a mind to do." As I have suggested elsewhere, my decision to follow an American trajectory may have been a reaction to the social and economic convulsions of the times. It occurs to me that the United States suddenly loomed as the last democratic bastion in the world after the German occupation of France in 1940. About then, I began to feel that it might be almost as important to understand American civilization as to preserve it. My hopes for a European reeducation and for extended *Wanderjahre* in storied places had dissolved by 1939, but I was already half convinced that given my ignorance of foreign tongues, it was too late for me to barge into nonanglophone cultures as I had once hoped to do. It says something about my state of mind in this free-floating period that instead of settling on a time-tried program of study, I would sign up for an ad hoc safari through some unchartered areas of "American civilization."

Under the flexible requirements of Harvard's interdepartmental degree, I could legitimately reconnoiter the byways of American social and intellectual thought without feeling pressure to become an authority on anything. The "Americanist" I invented would know something about many things bearing on American history and society. He would compound a goulash of his civilization from old lecture notes; from books and articles on church history, geography, education, political thought, and popular culture; from conversations with representative men and women; and, most of all, from the musings of American writers, famous and obscure. This all-purpose synthesizer never materialized, but following his track opened areas new to me and, more important, gave me an excuse to hop grasshopper-fashion from one topic to another.

I left Harvard in 1939, a putative historian about to get down to writing his doctoral dissertation. The finished product was an economic, political, and cultural examination of an American community (Cincinnati, Ohio) in the age of Andrew Jackson (1819–38). It was my critique of Frederick Jackson Turner's "frontier thesis," and it was an experiment to test the generalizations in Alexis de Tocqueville's *Democracy in America.* Written in what I hoped was a philosophical spirit, it reflected in essence my socioeconomic biases and analyzed affirmatively a buoyant and dynamic society. When completed, it was accepted without a request for revision and without enthusiasm. Until its publication fifty years later, I didn't know that it had been called an interlibrary-loan classic and a pioneer work in urban history.

Long before then, I had given up the expectation of developing into a proper historian, even as I continued to attend meetings of genuine historians and to hang on their table talk. To show off my bona fides (and spurred by the prospect of making some money), I coauthored an American history textbook with Richard Hofstadter and William Miller—the first a political and cultural historian and the most acclaimed of our trio, the second a toughminded economic and business historian familiar with the nuts and bolts of the publishing industry. *The United States: The History of the Republic* (1957) took three years to write and, once written, more time to keep up to date and in good repair. Without Hofstadter's name, I doubt if our book would have sold as well as it did. Happily, it hit the market during a lull between the old and the new competition, and its flood of adoptions paid for the college educations of my three sons. Its opening sentence (my contribution) was "America has been discovered many times."

Our success did not delude me into believing that I belonged to the historian's guild. I was too distracted by the historical trees (memoirs, private letters, anecdotes, gossip, and the like)—too literary—to see the woods. During the next fifty years, I filled in some of the empty spaces on my map of America by reviewing scholarly and popular works on subjects that were often new or unfamiliar to me. I labored over the tone and style of these pieces and sometimes committed what the poet Allen Tate called the young critic's chronic sin—intimating a knowledge he doesn't possess. I had no agenda. I took on jobs as they turned up, with little thought of what I might be letting myself in for.

It astonishes me now how casually I entered into the risky, time-consuming assignment of editing the diary of Arthur Crew Inman. Roughly twelve to fifteen million words in length and packaged in over 150 typed manuscript volumes, it took six years to reduce it to less than a tenth of its original bulk. I was well paid, but I quickly regretted my decision, depressed by the sheer magnitude of the task and by the spoiled, prejudiced, manipulative, sadomasochistic, self-pitying author. Sequestered for a good part of his life in the heavily curtained room of a seedy Boston apartment hotel, Inman spent decades chronicling the history of his times and himself for posterity. Newspaper items, books, and radio broadcasts furnished part of what he called his "diary fodder," but mostly he fed on the life stories of the hundreds of men and women who answered his advertisements for paid "talkers" (he had plenty of time and money) willing to submit to his relentless interrogations.

Many reviewers of my two-volume abridgement were so put off by Inman's outrageous racial and religious prejudices that they did less than justice, I thought, to the self-defined "bastard gazetteer" and his four-decade report of the American scene. The detestable sick soul had his mitigating decencies, and I felt a certain obligation to show him at his literary best. My haphazard excursions into American history and literature (not to mention the fact that Inman's diary covered a period of years in my own lifetime) made me, in my own eyes, a legitimate interpreter of the man and the moment. Editing the diary helped me to put into perspective "the long foreground," as Emerson would say, of my own career. It widened the scope of my camera eye and added something strange and novel to the American canon. In the end, I treated it as a challenging exercise, rather like uncovering an unusual specimen buried in acres of shale, but of no less importance to me than the three books that preceded it and that drew me further into native grounds: *Men of Good Hope* (1951), *Writers on the Left* (1961) and *The Unwritten War* (1973).

Men of Good Hope was gently received and qualifiedly commended for its style and "valuable contributions," but some reviewers found it hard to believe that "prophetic agitators" as diverse as Emerson, Theodore Parker, Edward Bellamy, William Dean Howells, Henry Demarest Lloyd, Thorstein Veblen, and Brooks Adams could share a common social outlook. What united them despite their differences, I argued unpersuasively, and what compelled my intense interest in them was their belief in the possibility of a cooperative society, their trust in the voting masses and in middle-class decencies, and their hatred of plutocracy. This was a hard sell, even for me. To many in the 1950s, the terms *middle-class* and *radicalism* connoted contrary values, so my brief for "progressivism" as a blend of utopian theory, Protestant theology, and pragmatic realism that eschewed any sentimentalizing of the proletariat probably puzzled or disconcerted a portion of my limited audience. Richard Hofstadter wrote me that I had confirmed his "liberal-conservative-elitist-ethical brand of private socialism" and gotten "the ethical-utopian element back into the center of things." David Riesman gave *Men of Good Hope* a thoughtful and penetrating appraisal, and Mary McCarthy, somewhat to my surprise, wrote to me that she fancied my chapter on William Dean Howells. But the book had small appeal for most professional historians or teachers of American literature. Most of my middle-class reformers, as Riesman observed, had "sunk nearly out of general circulation." An irregular in the ranks of the non-Communist Left, I did not fit neatly into any political party and had no taste or talent for polemics.

Writers on the Left was published six years after the decline and fall of Senator Joseph McCarthy. His ghost still haunted the hearts of his victims and his minions, none more so than Arthur Inman, who had grieved when he learned of McCarthy's death. Yes, Inman conceded, McCarthy was a rough fellow, even a demagogue, but then weren't FDR and Truman—even Abraham Lincoln—demagogic at times? My episodic study of American literature and Communism was welcomed in some quarters as a message to harassed ex-Reds that at last they could come out of the cold without fear of retribution. I had no such thought in mind when I wrote it, but apparently a number of veterans of the Communist movement had been surprised and relieved by its nonaccusatory tone. There are no villains in *Writers on the Left*; no unbridgeable gulf divides "them" from "us." The radicals in its pages range from old-stock rebels, reformers, anarchists, and progressives to the children of recent immigrants. I gave examples of what I took to be their solemn and ridiculous zealotries, but mainly I chose to show them as citizens of an America still open to dissent and with a permeable class structure. I wanted to single out some of the artists, writers, and public figures, past and present, who belonged to my company of nonconformists and who exemplified what I liked best about the American radical tradition. So to me, at least, *Writers on the Left* is a patriotic book.

The same could be said for *The Unwritten War* (1973), my covert offering to the America I constructed from books, to the American landscape, and to the writers and critics and teachers who educated and befriended me. It probably would have remained unwritten had not the energetic historian and biographer Allan Nevins invited me to contribute a volume to a series he was planning on the social and cultural impact of the Civil War.

A voluminous reader of English and American literature, he was particularly keen on having the literary responses to the war fill a major slot in his project. His death before my book was half done shut off a flow of learning of great importance to me, but while he lived, I profited from our intermittent walks and talks.

The title of *The Unwritten War* provoked reviewers. How could a war said to be "unwritten" have inspired libraries of books and have remained uninterruptedly a national obsession? *The Unwritten War* got good notices, but its argument that the Civil War was not so much effaced as unfaced and that our writers failed to acknowledge the centrality of racial fear (not slavery itself, but black slavery) as the root cause of the conflict, didn't find many takers. One taker was Ralph Ellison, friend, author, and neighbor, who read *The Unwritten War* before its publication and accepted its burden tout court. As he put it, "with few exceptions," American writers "sought to escape the artistic and philosophical challenges" posed by the war. For Edmund Wilson, however, race was a peripheral issue. We had often discussed Civil War literature and history at the time when a spate of his essay reviews of books touching directly or indirectly on the war were appearing in the *New Yorker*. Eventually, he incorporated these pieces ("dress rehearsals," he called them) in his masterpiece *Patriotic Gore* (1962). Had he lived long enough to read my book, he would have disputed its thesis, for he was riding his own hobbyhorse—namely, the notion that the American Civil War was a "biological and geological phenomenon" and the consequence of a national mania and repulsive enthusiasms. I took this to be the burden of his rather explosive *Patriotic Gore* introduction, which seemed simplistic and far-fetched on first reading and which Stuart Hughes and I urged him to omit or to publish separately. Four decades later, I find Wilson's withering comments on the contrast between national words and actions to the point and in keeping with his prickly patriotism, with his disdain of "warlike cant" and of the "God bless America" brand of national piety.

I started life as an exemplary "American boy," unrebellious and cheerfully receptive to everything I was taught or read. I honored the statesmen and soldiers and inventors looking out of my schoolbooks or featured in *The American Boy* or *Boy's Life*. I chanted the Pledge of Allegiance to the United States (the "under God" provision had yet to be tacked on) and recited the Boy Scout Oath, with its injunction to be brave, clean, and reverent. Yet even during this interlude of cultural indoctrination, I was steeped in the lowbrow and irreverent popular culture that washed around me. The distance between them had narrowed by the time I enrolled in Harvard's program in the history of American civilization, and I was already seeing myself as an extra in a history pageant of my times. Like the child in Whitman's poem, I "went forth" every day to incorporate myself in the unfolding land, and although I never thought of myself as a "kosmos" or as emerging from a sequence of Edens and compost heaps, as Walt did, I could and did respond in my own fashion to the landscapes in *Leaves of Grass*. The Walt I latched onto was a double man: the patriot exhorter of "These States" and the ironical realist, veteran of public and personal disasters.

I associated the first Walt with young America at takeoff point and with the seventeenth- and eighteenth-century promoters who hyperbolically advertised the New World's lush fertility. He took immense satisfaction in American plenitude, and so did I. I remember my quiet joy when I found in an 1823 issue of *Niles Register* a list of reasons for the inevitable glory of the Republic: we were blessedly independent of all foreign nations; our government was the freest and most liberal that ever existed; our national debt was paltry, our citizenry untrammeled, and our territory spacious enough to contain "all the superfluous population of Europe."

I thought the second Walt downplayed the idyll of a democratic Cockaigne. The United States he surveyed and diagnosed in *Democratic Vistas* (1871) was suffering from a "deep disease." In that jeremiad, the loving but stern physician lists the symptoms of civic corruption at a moment of unprecedented "materialistic advancement": the late war has secured the Union, yet society in the United States is "canker'd, crude, superstitious, and rotten"; a plethora of churches and sects ("dismal phantoms," he calls them) "usurp the name of religion." Whitman likens business (an "all-devouring word") to the "magician's serpent" that has gobbled up the other serpents and remains "sole master of the field." He maintains that the "depravity of the business class" is much greater than supposed and that "the cities reek with respectable as much as non-respectable robbery and scoundrelism." According to the Whitman of *Democratic Vistas*, democracy in the United States, purportedly destined for greatness, could turn out to be "the most tremendous failure of our time."

I analogized Whitman's darker America in the scenes of social misery that I had observed during the Great Depression and in the culture of dissent I fed on. But it is likely that reading American literature and history most affected my social vision, as I gathered facts and figures on the origins of great American fortunes, on racial bigotry, on labor struggles and political corruption, and on the wasteful exploitation of national resources. I reacted almost viscerally to chronicles of ecological disaster—carrier pigeons slaughtered to extinction, buffalo herds exterminated, lakes and rivers polluted, hardwood forests scythed, prairie topsoil (which had taken centuries to accrue) blown away in storms of dust.

An English friend of long duration once offered me a gloss on my pained reaction to these stories of nature vandalized. As an American of recent immigrant origin, I was making a claim on what he called "a retrospective birthright." He reckoned that I had spent a good part of my life in search of a "cultural genealogy" and for ways to attach myself to those parts of the American tradition that I valued and respected; and so I had. He might have added, but didn't, that my social dissensions hadn't been "radical" in the root-and-branch meaning of that word and that I had never committed myself unreservedly to the principles and programs of the titans I wrote about.

Now I find myself a citizen of two Americas. One of them is the country of Uncle Sam, an America, in the words of Herman Melville, "intrepid, unprincipled, reckless, predatory, with boundless ambition, civilized in the externals but savage at heart." The other is its blssed double, home of heroes and clowns and of the cheerful and welcoming democratic collective—"the place where I was born." For all of my romantic satanism and the satisfaction I took and still take in the doctrine of original sin, it is this second America to which I feel culturally and temperamentally attuned.

INDEX

Text design by Mary H. Sexton
Typesetting by Delmastype, Ann Arbor, Michigan

The text font is Adobe Caslon. William Caslon released
his first typefaces in 1722. Caslon's types became popular
throughout Europe and the American colonies; printer
Benjamin Franklin hardly used any other typeface.
The first printings of the American Declaration of
Independence and the Constitution were set in Caslon.
For her Caslon revival, designer Carol Twombly studied
specimen pages printed by William Caslon between
1734 and 1770.

—courtesy adobe.com

Franklin Gothic, one of the most popular sans serif
types ever produced, was designed by Morris Fuller
Benton in 1902 for American Type Founders. In 1979,
under license with ATF, Vic Caruso began work on
more weights of the design for ITC. In 1991, David
Berlow completed the family for ITC by creating
compressed and condensed weights. It is featured
here for the title.

—courtesy adobe.com